When Catholics Speak about Jews:

NOTES FOR HOMILISTS AND CATECHISTS

John T. Pawlikowski • James A. Wilde

Liturgy Training Publications

Printed in the United States of America

ISBN 0–930467–60–4

Design by Elizandro Carrington

Contents

Introduction

With only a few short paragraphs, the Second Vatican Council, on 28 October 1965, committed Catholicism to reverse the direction of a nineteen-century-old relationship with Jewish people. *Nostra Aetate*, the council's *Declaration on the Relation of the Church to Non-Christian Religions,* pointed a new direction for all Catholics. No longer acceptable was John Chrysostom's advice for relations with the Jews: "Don't greet them; don't even discuss anything with them." From 1965 on, Catholics are encouraged to deepen their understanding and appreciation of Jews, especially "by way of biblical and theological inquiry and through friendly discussion" (#4).

Alas, not all Catholics got the point. Children can still participate in liturgical celebrations in American churches and get the distinct impression that Jews are somehow responsible for Jesus' death, that Jewish people fare less well before God than we luckier Christians do, and that "the Old Testament teaches law and sin but the New Testament mercy and love." Stereotypes about Jews from poorly informed parents still go unchallenged in our schools and catechetical programs. And some potential adult catechumens or candidates for full communion with the Catholic church still express bewilderment about how a church which strives to be Christian can conduct itself so carelessly regarding Jews.

Some observers consider the development of better Catholic-Jewish relations in the final one-third of the twentieth century as the "litmus test" for measuring Vatican II's overall effectiveness. We fail this test if someone attends an Eastertime liturgy, for example, and concludes from some words of the first reading from the Acts of the Apostles that Catholics still believe "You [Jews] put to death the Author of Life" (Acts 3:15; Third Sunday of Easter, cycle B). We fail also if a visitor comes with us on the Twenty-seventh Sunday of Ordinary Time in cycle A, listens to the parable of the tenants in the vineyard who killed the owner's son (Matthew 21:33-43), and learns in the homily that the Jews or their leaders were these cruel tenants. Examples are many.

For the catechist or homilist working from the lectionary, the problems are not simple but complex and multifaceted. First, there are problems within the biblical texts themselves. The authors of the Christian Scriptures—by no means neutral in their approach to history—sometimes use hyperbole and occasionally reflect in their words an underlying one-sidedness on issues, or even rank prejudice, just as the authors of the Hebrew Scriptures do. Second, the committees and consultants responsible for the 1969 lectionary had their own presuppositions and methods. For example, as the reader will learn, the promise/fulfillment themes reflected in the lectionary selections particularly in Advent needlessly constrain the biblical message and leave delicate issues wide open to serious misinterpretation. Third, at times preachers and catechists do not have the background required to use these texts accurately, creatively or even faithfully. And finally, members of the assembly have their own prejudices and may not even be aware that there is a problem.

Sensitivities need sharpening. Consciousness needs raising. Prejudice needs confronting. Some of the biblical texts cry out for explanations which they seldom receive. And sometimes the interpretations they get makes matters even worse. Vatican II's voice has not yet been heard throughout the land.

This book was written to advance one more step the cause of *Nostra Aetate*. We want to give preachers and teachers some practical, usable insights in dealing with the biblical texts sensitively and fruitfully in homilies and discussions. The authors know that in the relations between Jews and Christians tearing down old walls and building new bridges takes a long time. One homily or one discussion is only a beginning. Therefore we want to heighten our readers' awareness and stimulate their renewed efforts, but we also want to support their patience. We think the issue merits all three.

Part 1 contains four articles by John T. Pawlikowski, Ph.D., corresponding to four times in the liturgical year. These explore the homiletic and catechetical problems and goals in matters that affect Catholic attitudes towards Judaism. Pawlikowski, a priest of the Servite Order and professor of Christian social ethics at Chicago Theological Union, is an articulate spokesperson and internationally known writer for Jewish-Christian relations. A member of the Catholic Bishops' Secretariat for Catholic-Jewish Relations, he has authored *Christ in the Light of Christian Jewish Dialogue* and eight other books on this and related social issues. As Pawlikowski makes clear, the difficulty is not always a matter of misunderstanding. At times the problems are in the scriptures themselves and in the use to which the lectionary puts them.

In part 2, James A. Wilde, Ph.D., makes some useful pedagogical points for religious educators, homilists, teachers and catechists as they work with the lectionary texts. Wilde, a New Testament interpreter and religious historian, is editor at Liturgy Training Publications. He shows that careful attention to the biblical texts in their literary and social context can clarify issues in Jewish-Christian relations before difficulties arise.

Part 3 offers several sample homilies, illustrations and bulletin announcements to stimulate creative use of the biblical texts in a manner that is sensitive both to the Jewish-Christian issue and to the attitudes of church goers. The sample homilies were prepared by John T. Pawlikowski, Gerard S. Sloyan and Robert B. Sherman. Sloyan, a priest and professor of Christian theology at Temple University, is known throughout the world for his prolific writing in the areas of liturgy and New Testament. Sherman, a priest of the diocese of St. Petersburg, is a gifted student of Judaica and exercises part of his ministry as counselor for Gulf Coast Jewish Family Services. The Sundays chosen for these sample homilies illustrate several facets of the problems faced by the preacher.

The samples which follow in part 3 include petitions for General Intercessions by James Wilde. They follow closely the words and images used in the lectionary for the day, but they may be adapted for other occasions. The reflections and illustrations may also be used flexibly as the need arises. Gabe Huck, who wrote many of them, serves as director of Liturgy Training Publications. The sample bulletin items can help to raise consciousness on Jewish-Christian relations over periods of time.

Finally, in part 4, there is a chronology of official and semi-official church statements on Jewish-Christian relations along with a summary of some of these statements. A comparison of the statements follows to show how a tradition is gradually unfolding in the church.

This book is therefore not just for preachers and teachers. It is for lectors, people who write introductions to biblical readings, people who compose General Intercessions for eucharistic celebrations. It is also for catechumenate teams, members of Bible study groups and any Christians who want to become better informed about how to handle complex scriptural texts on the delicate matter of Jewish-Christian relations. This book is about healing a relationship through the kind of preaching and teaching demanded by Vatican II.

PART ONE

Jewish People In Christian Preaching And Teaching

John T. Pawlikowski

Advent: Rethinking the Fulfillment Theme

Promises and Preludes?

The readings from the prophets selected for the three cycles seem to push the hearers of the word in one common direction—the Jesus whose coming we celebrate at Christmas is the fulfillment of the message of hope and promise the prophets proclaimed. Under this line of thinking Jesus' birth is viewed as the inauguration of the "days to come" described by Isaiah in the A cycle and Jeremiah in the C cycle (First Sunday of Advent).

Sections of these readings can easily leave the impression that pre-Jesus Israel was guilt-ridden and in mourning, eagerly awaiting its liberation. We listen in the C cycle (Second Sunday of Advent) to Baruch's summons to Jerusalem to "take off your robe of mourning and misery," or in the B cycle to Isaiah speaking about the anticipated, imminent expiation of Jerusalem's guilt. It is very difficult for the average Catholic worshiper, conditioned for so long by stereotypes of Judaism's spiritual vapidity and notions of Jewish suffering as punishment, not to imagine that Jesus' coming marked the liberation of people from the emptiness and sinfulness of Judaism.

When Isaiah in cycle A complains about the house of David "wearying" God himself, when Zephaniah in cycle C tells us that the Lord has removed the judgment against Jerusalem, and when Isaiah again (at Midnight Mass) speaks of the people "who walked in darkness," this sense of overriding Jewish guilt intensifies. The impression can easily be drawn from these readings, and often is by homilists, that Judaism was incapable of any spiritual regeneration short of the emergence of the messiah who is clearly identified with Jesus.

The way the readings have been selected and arranged also leads us to believe that the prophets clearly foresaw the details of Jesus' birth and that their words were primarily directed to this event. On the Fourth Sunday of Advent in cycle C we hear Micah speak of the ruler of Israel coming from Bethlehem-Ephrathah. And there are references in the readings of all the cycles to King David and to a virgin giving birth. The subtle message seems to be that anyone who knew the Hebrew Scriptures ought to have recognized Jesus as the expected Jewish messiah.

In Advent, preachers and catechists confront a basic problem here. The implied exegesis of these prophetic texts as they have been set up by the framers of the liturgy stands in tension with what many biblical theologians and writers on christology are saying. Leading scripture scholars have clearly repudiated the notion that the prophets in these readings were expressly speaking about the birth of Jesus. John L. McKenzie is one who has made this point in decisive language:

> This writer has said elsewhere that Jesus is the Messiah of Judaism, and that he can be understood only as Messiah of Judaism. I stand by this observation, but I do not believe that it obliges me to find faith in Jesus Messiah in the Old Testament. Jesus transformed the ideal of Messiah when he fulfilled it. The total reality of Jesus Messiah is found nowhere in the Old Testament, not even in its totality. (*A Theology of the Old Testament*, pp. 31-32)

The misguided interpretations of the prophets as directly foretelling the coming of Christ is really part of a general Christian misuse of the Hebrew Scriptures. We in the church have tended to look on the Hebrew Scriptures only as prelude, only as giving us glimpses of the New Testament message. We have generally failed to appreciate its spiritual richness in its own right. There exists a mandate for Catholics to move away from this narrow approach to the Hebrew Scriptures which not only leads to negative portrayals of Judaism but hampers our own spiritual development. This direction is clear from the recent words of Pope John Paul II. Speaking to the Jewish community at Mainz, West Germany, the Pope recalled a statement of Vatican Council II. In its Declaration on the Church and the Jewish People, the council insisted that "effort must be made to understand better everything in the Old Testament that has its own, permanent value . . . since this value is not wiped out by the later interpretations of the New Testament."

If we then examine most major works of systematic christology today, we find that in their interpretations of the Christ-event there is little reliance on the "fulfillment of Old Testament prophecies" motif that so dominates the Advent liturgy. The theologians are aware of where scripture scholars have gone on the question.

In the final analysis only a major reworking of the Advent liturgy to bring it more into conformity with the findings of contemporary exegesis will permanently undercut the potential for falsely stereotyping biblical Judaism. Some liturgists are aware of the problem and it is certainly urgent that they join with scripture scholars and theologians to address it. The poetry and beauty of the texts must be preserved, but that is exactly what can happen if they are freed (we are freed) of an interpretation which needs to find fulfillment everywhere.

The Prophet's Task

While the ultimate solution to the problem is beyond the homilist and catechist, there are definite possibilities for preaching and catechizing on the

Advent texts that will lessen their anti-Semitic potential. First of all, emphasis should be placed on the fact that the prophets were speaking first and foremost to the people of their own day. Their concern was not to foretell the future nor to announce the advent of Christ. Speaking in the name of God, the root meaning of the term "prophet," and with divine authority, they were reminding the people of the obligations of their covenant. They realized that God and God's people had become estranged through human unfaithfulness. They hoped to overcome the alienation by reminding people of the dire consequences if they ignored the message, but they also recalled that there could be a new fullness of divine help if the people would turn away from their sin.

Jewish and Christian Responses

The second point we need to emphasize is that an adequate response to the prophetic call was not totally delayed until the coming of Jesus. The rebuilding of the Temple and the rapid growth of the pharisaic movement during the Second Temple (or intertestamental) period are clear illustrations of the seriousness with which the people of Israel took the prophets' warnings. They knew they had endured exile as a punishment for unfaithfulness. Following the lead of the prophets, many were determined that this painful experience would never be repeated.

The period in which Jesus was born and preached was not one in which Judaism was spiritually bankrupt. Some Jews hoped for a political messiah who would liberate them from the political oppression of the Roman conquerors of Palestine. Others, like the Pharisees, turned their attention to the total rebuilding of the daily life and spirit of the Jewish people. Jesus was part of this effort, though he had some distinctive ideas not shared by other Jews. (I develop this in my recent book, *Christ in Light of the Christian-Jewish Dialogue*, published by Paulist Press.)

The Second Temple period was for both Judaism and the newly born Christian community a time when the prophetic promise of a new inrush of divine grace was being realized. It was not invalid for the gospel writers to speak of the coming of Jesus within the framework of traditional prophetic categories of judgment/promise. Jesus certainly represents in Christian eyes a new outpouring of divine help, the promise of human salvation. In his ministry and in his person the alienation between God and people which so concerned the prophets was being overcome. But it would be just as legitimate to apply these words to the regeneration efforts underway in Judaism at the same time. While church and synagogue eventually found it necessary to go their separate ways, they both represented serious and constructive, though somewhat different, responses to the earlier call of the

4

prophets for renewed faithfulness. Contrary to popular belief in the church, it was not only the Christian community which was responsive to the words of Isaiah, Jeremiah, Baruch and others.

Emmanuel

Thirdly, preaching and catechesis in Advent can and must emphasize the centrality of the incarnation. It is a unique doctrine developed from the preaching and ministry of Jesus, even though there already existed in Second Temple Judaism a growing sense of God's intimacy with humanity. But belief in the incarnation does not automatically invalidate the continuing meaningfulness of Judaism. However theologians eventually restate the theological relationship between the two faith communities (a process that is still in its infancy), the basic point remains that from a Christian perspective both traditions retain a central value. This view has been clearly affirmed by the Vatican Council and by the recent popes.

Christianity considers God's intervention in Christ to be decisive, but (and this must be stressed) this intervention did not represent the coming of the messianic kingdom in the Jewish sense. This is the point made by McKenzie. If Jesus is the messiah, it is in a transformed sense and hence Judaism was not "blind" in not recognizing a connection between Jesus and the messianic kingdom. Increasingly Christian theology has placed strong emphasis on the "not yet" dimension of the Christ-event. The messianic kingdom for both Jews and Christians still lies ahead. As we wait together and as we work together, the prophetic selections read during Advent can become a new summons to the church to reach out to the Jewish people and recognize them as partners in the building of the kingdom.

Such cooperation is especially timely with respect to the imperative of justice. Though this theme is highlighted much more in the readings from Isaiah used in the A cycle than it is in the C cycle, there is no reason why it cannot be raised in other years as a way of urging Catholics to join Jews in a common response to this prophetic call. Pope John Paul II spoke directly to this in his German address. "Jews and Christians, as children of Abraham, are called to be a blessing for the world (cf. Genesis 12:2ff) by committing themselves together for peace and justice among all persons and peoples."

Since from the Christian perspective both Jews and Christians share in the covenant relationship with God (cf. Romans 11:29), only by working together can we bring about the full realization of the final messianic kingdom. This should be made clear in our preaching and catechesis in Advent. Jews are not antagonists, but partners, in the messianic dream we celebrate during the Advent/Christmas season.

Lent: Jesus' "New" Word

The Influence of Judaism on Jesus

The liturgical readings for the lenten season (prior to Palm Sunday) repeat many of the same difficulties over and over again. When the Christian assembly hears Matthew speak about "hypocrites in the synagogue" in the Ash Wednesday liturgy, or Jesus' words about destroying the Temple in the B cycle reading from John on the Third Sunday of Lent, or the description of Jesus' supposed conflict with the Pharisees in the C cycle reading from Luke on the Fourth Sunday, there is a great likelihood they will imagine that the Judaism of Jesus' day was largely devoid of spiritual depth. References to earlier divine punishments of the Jewish people, such as those mentioned by Paul in the passage from 1 Corinthians read on the Third Sunday of Lent in cycle C, further intensify the negative image of Judaism.

In the same manner, prophetic texts such as Joel (Ash Wednesday), Jeremiah on the "new covenant" (B cycle, Fifth Sunday) and Isaiah on God doing something new (C cycle, Fifth Sunday) open the way for additional subtle distortions. These speak of Judaism as completely fulfilled by the Christ-event, a misrepresentation prominent during the Advent season discussed above.

The problem for the homilist and catechist should now be clear: How can one positively overcome the direct and indirect potential for anti-Judaism that realistically exists in the Advent and lenten readings. Put another way, how does the homilist or catechist present the basic message of the scriptures to Christians in a way that allows them to develop a constructive attitude toward the continued vitality of the Jewish people and to recognize the central influence of the Jewish tradition on the teachings of Jesus?

Key to achieving such a goal is a proper understanding of what was "new" in the word as proclaimed by Jesus. A common Christian assumption, frequently made by homilists and catechists, is that it was all new, that Judaism was the "old" that had to be discarded because it had become hopelessly corrupt. Temple/synagogue, Torah, the Pharisees — these all became negative symbols for a great many Christians, representing the exact opposite of the authentic, liberating spirituality found in Christ through the church.

The biblical scholars of several decades tell us that any simplistic contrast between the "new" of Jesus' message and the "old" of Judaism is fundamentally inaccurate. Judaism was the spiritual center of Jesus' message, not its devilish opponent. The "newness" of Jesus' message grew out of the overall renewal of the covenant tradition called for by Jeremiah. This renewal process was central to the Judaism of Jesus' time. The Christian biblical scholar Carl G. Howie has written that the period between the two testaments was ". . . most active politically, intellectually, and spiritually . . . It was an active, creative era both in the one world of political struggles and in the fragmented world of man's inner life . . . Much happened in these four centuries, and one must understand these happenings if he wishes to comprehend the meaning of the New Testament" (*The Creative Era*, pages 9-10).

Jesus and the Renewal of the Pharisees

The creativity of this period produced two new religious movements, pharisaic/rabbinic Judaism and the Christian church. Each had many subgroups. While church and synagogue eventually split into two distinctive entities and while that split took place within an atmosphere of considerable antagonism, we can no longer doubt that they shared a deep, binding spiritual center. Though Jesus advanced some pharisaic notions in ways no longer acceptable to the vast majority of the movement, he continued to affirm many of their most central religious insights.

This continued bond with the Jewish tradition is brought out somewhat subtly but very importantly in the transfiguration accounts of Matthew, Mark and Luke which are read on the Second Sunday of Lent. Just as the Pharisees were intent in linking their renewal of the covenant tradition with Mosaic authority, so the gospel writers, in the same spirit, established this connection with respect to Jesus' efforts. We often focus on the "miracle" dimensions of these accounts while missing the vital link between Jesus' teaching and the Mosaic tradition which the accounts affirm and which would have been very clear to the original hearers of Jesus' word.

The assertion that Jesus shared in the process of renewing the covenant tradition within pharisaism may strike many as strange given the overwhelmingly negative image the movement has had in Christian preaching. Pharisees have generally been presented as the archenemies of Jesus, people who stood for everything Jesus was against. Recent Christian and Jewish scholarship, while leaving many details about pharisaism still unanswered, has begun to develop a much more constructive image of the movement (cf., for example, Ellis Rivkin's *A Hidden Revolution: The Pharisees' Search for the Kingdom Within*).

The supposed battles between Jesus and the Pharisees in the synoptic gospels are seen more clearly now as commonplace, internal pharisaic disagreements; pharisaism embraced many differing and disagreeing subgroups. The 1973 statement from the French Bishops' Commission on Relations with Jews speaks to the issue with great clarity.

Contrary to established ways of thinking, it must be emphasized that pharisaic doctrine is not opposed to that of Christianity. The Pharisees sought to make the Law come alive in every Jew, by interpreting its commandments in such a way as to adapt them to the various spheres of life. Contemporary research has shown that the Pharisees were no more strangers to the innermost meaning of the Law than were the masters of the Talmud.

This creative dimension of pharisaism and its links with Jesus' efforts at covenant renewal must be borne in mind by the homilist when accounts of the pharisaic-Jesus relationship appear in the Fourth Sunday reading from Luke in cycle C or the Fourth Sunday reading from John in cycle A.

At the core of the pharisaic revolution in which Jesus participated lay a new perception of the relationship between God and people, a perception far more personal and intimate than any envisioned by previous movements within Judaism. This change in outlook was so dramatic that the Pharisees were impelled to devise new titles to describe God. One of the principal names they applied to God was "father." As it was developed by the Pharisees, the father image made people aware of a new intimacy between God and the individual person.

This sense of divine-human intimacy subverted the earlier priestly/Temple system in Judaism which was based on heredity and convinced that only a handful of select people were sufficiently holy to approach God in a direct fashion. Inevitably this "spiritual" transformation led to a complete reshaping of the liturgical, ministerial and institutional life of Second Temple Judaism. The Christian church can, in a way, be understood as one important product of this renewal. Along with its sister institution, the synagogue, it represented a significantly new way of organizing the communal life of the religious assembly in which equality and concern for justice and mercy prevailed. Though church and synagogue eventually found it necessary to go their separate ways, their common origin as creative replacements for the restricted, elitist Temple system should never be forgotten.

In addition to the link between church and synagogue, evident connections between Jesus and pharisaism can be found in the style of ministry each adopted, in their willingness to reinterpret the Torah to meet new demands of their own time, and in their ethical outlooks (the Sermon on the Mount is imbued with pharisaic spirituality). Links can likewise be found in their emphasis on liturgy within the communal meal of the community and in their belief in the resurrection of the individual.

The Distinct Word of Jesus

Our basic question remains: What is new in the word of Jesus? We find the answer not in simple opposition to Judaism, especially its pharisaic version. Rather, he pushed the basic pharisaic understanding of the profound intimacy between God and the individual person beyond what any branch of pharisaism was prepared to acknowledge. The differences that exist between Jesus and the Pharisees generally revolve around this issue and the concomitant importance of the dignity of the individual person.

One example of this is Jesus' own sense of the closeness between humanity and divinity experienced in his person. Jesus' "Abba experience," as the contemporary Catholic theologian Edward Schillebeeckx terms it, indicates a proximity to God that no Pharisees of the time were willing to grant, despite the movement's profound sense of God as father. The consciousness of a deep tie was certainly present in pharisaism, but notions of separation, of distance, remained firm in the minds of even its most liberal members.

Jesus was also far more willing to bend the requirements of Torah (which he basically endorsed) when an individual's well-being was at stake. Thus he got into some trouble with Pharisees over his healing of a man's diseased hand on the Sabbath. He did this, in the words of the late Christian scholar on Judaism James Parkes, "as an assertion of the primacy of each man as person" (*The Foundations of Judaism and Christianity,* p. 177). It is also possible that Jesus had a stronger commitment to the *am ha-aretz,* the people of the land, than most of pharisaism.

Another difference lay in Jesus' great emphasis on the immediacy of the kingdom's presence. Love of enemies was likewise an area where Jesus went beyond the prevailing pharisaic stress which, while rejecting outright hatred for an enemy, never insisted on the need to love one's enemies. The Israeli New Testament scholar David Flusser makes this point:

> It is clear that Jesus' moral approach to God and man . . . is unique and incomparable. According to the teachings of Jesus you have to love the sinners, while according to Judaism you have not to hate the wicked. It is important to note that the positive love even toward enemies is Jesus' personal message. We do not find this doctrine in the New Testament outside of the words of Jesus himself . . . In Judaism hatred is practically forbidden, but love to the enemy is not prescribed.

9

(''A New Sensitivity in Judaism and the Christian Message,'' *Harvard Theological Review,* April 1968, page 126)

Echoes of this attitude on the part of Jesus are visible in several of the lenten readings (for example, the gospel selection on the Fifth Sunday of Lent in cycle C).

Jesus' stress on the basic dignity of the human person led to a fuller vision of the link that exists, that has always existed, between God and humanity. Divinity and humanity stand in a much more intimate relationship than previous generations had thought possible. This linkage carries profound implications for human relationships as well as for the fundamental relationship between humanity and God. It also accords to each individual person a great sense of dignity.

This awareness was tied to the development of the heightened sense of the individual's worth so characteristic of the pharisaic revolution. Nonetheless, in the final analysis, we must admit that the christologies of John and the later Paul represent a significant advance in this area when compared to the understanding prevailing in Second Temple Judaism. This was the ''new'' word of Jesus that we remember during Lent and Easter. The bond between humanity and divinity cannot be broken by death; it is the root of the notion of resurrection. It is likewise the basis on which we can proclaim in faith the future fulfillment of the kingdom. One of its more important implications was the universalization of the covenant tradition in a way Judaism had not fully anticipated and was not completely prepared to accept despite the universalist thrust present in so much of its own biblical tradition and in the pharisaic movement itself.

The Full Remembering of Jesus

The Jesus who gave us the ''new'' word likewise was the one for whom the Sinai covenant remained at the core of spirituality. As church and synagogue split, Christianity frequently accepted only the new word of Jesus. In so doing it remembered only a skeletal Jesus. The Sinai covenant's deep commitment to a celebration of community, its understanding of the goodness of creation, its sense of the importance of history as a locus of salvation and the central role of the human person as God's co-creator were often undervalued in the church. Christian renewal today is recovering something of this lost heritage, so well preserved in Judaism.

As we proclaim and teach the word in Lent the prophetic readings can be used to help Christians evaluate their own commitment to the covenant tradition and the values it represents. Are we being faithful to the human dignity it implies? Do we have the same spirit of acceptance towards Jews and others that marked the conduct of Jesus? Lent has nothing to do with expressly or implicitly preaching Christianity as the fulfillment (or even worse, the elimination) of Judaism. Rather, we should examine how adequately the Jewish component of Jesus' spirituality has been integrated into the faith life of the church, and how often the lack of such integration has resulted in forms of anti-Semitism that have been roundly condemned by Vatican Council II and all recent popes.

Proclaiming the Passion: Division or Reconciliation

A Covenant Still Valid

Ever since Vatican Council II and its attempt to set Jewish-Catholic relations on a new footing the liturgies of Palm Sunday and Good Friday have proved to be a special problem for the homilist. Jewish friends have sometimes confided that it is the time of the year they dread most, for the media and the churches tend to be filled with talk that does little to enhance the image of Jews and Judaism.

Both the Vatican and the National Conference of Catholic Bishops have cautioned us about the need to be especially vigilant in our preaching and teaching of God's word when proclaiming the passion. The 1975 Vatican guidelines began to apply the general principles in the conciliar statement on relations with the Jewish people. They address this issue in bold language: "With respect to liturgical readings, care will be taken to see that homilies based on them will not distort their meaning, especially when it is a question of passages which seem to show the Jewish people in an unfavorable light." The document urges the homilist to help people understand the true interpretation of all such texts, assisting them to see ". . . the continuity of our faith with that of the earlier covenant . . . without minimizing those elements of Christianity which are original."

In November of 1975 the American bishops issued a document celebrating the tenth anniversary of the Vatican Council's declaration, *Nostra Aetate*. This strikes much the same chord regarding the obligations incumbent upon those charged with proclamation of the word. The bishops write: ". . . homilists and liturgists [should] pay special attention to the presentation and interpretation of scripture so as to promote among the Catholic people a genuine appreciation of the special place of the Jewish people as God's first-chosen in the history of salvation and in no way slight the honor and dignity that is theirs."

The mandate is thus clear: Christian preaching and teaching needs to free itself from the historic tendency to describe the significance of the death/resurrection of Christ as the antithesis of Judaism. Put another way, our people must be taught the continuing validity of the Jewish covenant which remains intact after the Christ event.

An End to "Jesus-Versus-Judaism" Preaching and Teaching

Fulfilling this mandate given us by the church will not be easy. Our people are accustomed to thinking of Christ as the total fulfillment of Judaism. Despite the Council's repudiation of the deicide charge many Catholics are still tainted in their attitudes toward Judaism by this fable. Popular culture with its *Jesus Christ Superstar* and *Godspell* has tended to reinforce the stereotype of collective Jewish responsibility for Jesus' death.

The point then is simply this: our Catholic communities need to be addressed forthrightly on this issue. Roundabout solutions will have little effect. And it needs to be made as plain as possible that we are not speaking of now exonerating Jews for the death of Christ or of changing our theology about the Easter event "to be nice to Jews." Whatever the basis for some of the past thinking in the church, a solid core of Christian biblical scholars has concluded that any theory of Jewish collective guilt for Jesus' death lacks historical foundation.

Historical accuracy, not exoneration, is thus the required emphasis in our preaching and teaching. These same biblical scholars have also shown us that changing our attitudes on this question will help us better appreciate the message of Jesus and the significance of the Easter event. For the Jewish tradition formed the context, not merely the backdrop, for Jesus' preaching and teaching. The Hebrew Scriptures were not just a prelude to it: they were the indispensable setting and spirit.

The stereotypical view of total antagonism between Jesus and the Jewish community not only distorts the image of the latter but also robs Christians of a full understanding of Jesus' actual teachings. The "benefits" to be gained by the church in burying once and for all the Jesus-versus-Judaism model for interpretation go beyond restoring Christian moral integrity after centuries of distorted signals on Jews (which many times led to their suffering and death). If we were to understand and speak about the continuity between Jesus and the progressive Jewish movements of his time we would enhance the richness of the church's Easter message.

Jesus with His People

In order to reorient Christian preaching and teaching during Palm Sunday and the Paschal Triduum from denunciations of Jews and Judaism several basic understandings must begin to grow among those entrusted with these ministries. First and foremost is the realization that Jesus in his proclamation of God's word — which brought him to the situation we remember at the Triduum — did not stand in opposition to the whole Jewish community of his day.

Far too often in the picture presented by Christians Jesus is a lone voice crying in the wilderness of massive legalism and spiritual shallowness among his people. Such a perspective stems in large part from the classical Christian attitude towards the misnamed "intertestamental" period (better called the Second Temple period). We have made this appear as a time when Judaism largely lost contact with the spiritual legacy of the Hebrew Scriptures. We now know that this is anything but the case.

Certainly there was legalism and corruption in Second Temple Judaism, expecially within the high priestly clique in Jerusalem. But these distortions of authentic Judaism were being denounced by new movements within Judaism such as pharisaism. Though Jesus' stance was unique in a number of crucial areas, his criticism of the spiritual/political leadership of the time was one shared by many of his Jewish brothers and sisters. The actual situation was not a simple "Jesus-against-them" (i.e., the entire Jewish community), but Jesus standing in concert with the progressive movements in Judaism such as the Pharisees over against the small group of Jews who were collaborators with the oppressive Roman authorities.

The Oppression of Jews Expressed in the Cross

We have some hint of the sympathetic link between Jesus and many Jews of his time in the passion reading from Mark: Joseph of Arimathea, a Pharisee and member of the Jewish court, asks Pilate for Jesus' body to give it proper burial. The contemporary Jewish historian Ellis Rivkin expresses this link as well as anyone. He says that "Who crucified Jesus?" needs to be replaced with "What crucified Jesus?" "Domination, tyranny, dictatorship, power and disregard for the life of others," says Rivkin, were the forces responsible. "If there were among them Jews who abetted such a regime, then they too shared the responsibility. The mass of Jews, however, who were so bitterly suffering under Roman domination that they were to revolt in but a few years against its tyranny, can hardly be said to have crucified Jesus. In the crucifixion their own plight of helplessness, humiliation and subjection was clearly written on the cross itself."

Even though Christians and Jews will interpret the ultimate theological significance of the passion differently, on one level the cross may be seen as a center of unity between Jesus and the progressive forces in Judaism in his time and between Christians and Jews today. It need not be the source of division it has been for so long. Making the connection between the suffering and death of Jesus and the sufferings endured by the Jewish people should be an important aspect of the Easter mystery.

The Passion Told by John

The passion narrative of Mark which is read on Palm Sunday of cycle B can rather easily be interpreted in accord with the orientation just outlined. But on Good Friday, John's account of Jesus' arrest and death presents greater difficulties. There has been considerable discussion of the fourth gospel's antagonism to Judaism in biblical and theological circles. John's use of the term "the Jews" in place of more particular names and his seeming identification of "the Jews" with the forces of utter darkness are at the center of this study. No consensus has yet emerged among scholars, but some definite directions are beginning to surface. John is increasingly being viewed as at one and the same time the most pro- and most anti-Jewish of the gospels. His account includes some of the most positive statements about Jesus' Jewish roots to be found anywhere in the New Testament. These usually occur in what scholars consider the earlier strata in the present gospel text. The portions of the gospel which have later origins are the ones where Jews are described in negative tones.

The "Jewish guilt" appears greater in the Johannine passion narrative than it does in the Marcan version. This is due primarily to the more generalized term "Jews" in John which replaces the Marcan "leaders." Pilate is depicted as less of a culprit in John who also gives greater play to the abuse of Jesus by the "Jewish" crowds while Mark stresses his mistreatment by the Roman soldiers. These story changes may well reflect the fourth gospel's greater intention of fostering an anti-Jewish attitude among its hearers.

Whatever the origins of the anti-Judaism in John we must confront it. It does no good to pretend that it is not there. Leading Johannine scholars such as Raymond Brown (in his *The Community of the Beloved Disciple*, for example) are more and more insistent that contemporary Christians deal with the anti-Judaic tendency in this gospel. Brown is convinced that our pastoral task today is to make it clear to people that we cannot endorse or justify this Johannine contention about "the Jews."

A side issue also needs discussion. More and more we are witnessing dramatic renditions of the passion narratives on Palm Sunday and Good Friday. Special care must be exercised that the dramatizations do not have the effect of further intensifying the anti-Judaic components. Vigilance is necessary in this regard on the part of pastors and liturgical leaders.

Changing the distortions of Judaism and its role in the death of Jesus in popular consciousness will take a long time. It will be difficult to get across the principle stressed by Raymond Brown — anti-Judaism is no longer a moral theology for our day. Preachers and teachers need to raise these matters even to the point of repetition. No single approach will prove successful.

Freeing the Prophets

Another major area of concern revolves around the meaning of the readings from the Hebrew Scriptures, especially the prophets, during the final week of Lent and during the Paschal Triduum. The impression can easily be given that their sole function is to show how Christ's death/resurrection fulfilled them. It is important to stress here that the book of Isaiah is not read merely as a prelude to belief in Jesus, but as a source of living faith. The reading of the Hebrew Scriptures must therefore be presented as a source of ongoing meaning for our faith and not merely as "leading up" to the epistle/gospel selections.

Something even more important is at stake here. However we understand the uniqueness and the newness of Jesus' message, we need to gain the sense of its context. Theologians and scripture scholars are beginning to stress that the Christ event did not totally fulfill the Jewish messianic ideals. There is still a "not yet" that we Christians await along with Jews.

The Continuing Covenant

The above realizations (Jesus as one with his people, not with their antagonists, and the inadequacy of a "promise/fulfillment" approach to the prophets) lead us to a third crucial point. In the Chrism Mass and in the fifth reading at the Easter Vigil, Isaiah insists that the covenant with Israel is permanent, even though capable of rejuvenation. It is also a point emphasized by Paul in Romans 9—11. Taking Isaiah as ongoing revelation for us today, as he was for Jesus in his time, we must proclaim to our people the continuing nature of God's covenant with Israel. The Easter event, however it enhanced religious understanding, has not fundamentally altered this nature.

These then are the principal areas of concern that the homilist and catechist interested in presenting Christian-Jewish reconciliation rather than division need to take up:

- Jesus' link with the progressive Jewish forces in his time in opposing political/religious injustice
- the differences in the passion narratives, with the realization that whatever anti-Judaism exists in John is no longer authentic Christian proclamation today
- the non-fulfilled aspect of the Christ event leaves the Jewish covenant theologically intact and renders the Hebrew Scriptures a source of ongoing meaning for Christian believers at Easter

These points need great attention. After centuries of anti-Semitism, after the Nazi holocaust, we can do no less as faithful Christians.

Eastertime: Reflections on the Nascent Church and Judaism

The Eastertime readings have a joyous tone about them. True, we learn of the fear and sufferings of Peter, Paul, Stephen and other early church leaders as they attempt to express the new vision of divine reality they have experienced through Christ. But the dominant mood in the readings, and the mood that captures our spirits as we immerse ourselves in liturgical celebration during this season, is joyous and optimistic. Something new has dawned, people are beginning to grasp it, and increasing numbers, especially from the Gentile world, are associating themselves with the original community of Jesus' disciples.

The scriptural account of the church's infancy, related most comprehensively in the Acts of the Apostles which provides the first reading in the three cycles for all the Sundays of the Easter season (plus the feast of the Ascension) has the effect of rejuvenating the church's life today. These readings help us cut through centuries of ecclesiastical overlay. They return us, if only briefly, to the vitality and idealism of the initial gospel vision.

So most Christians would be rather surprised at the reaction of a rabbinic colleague of mine who attended Mass this Easter season. He has impeccable credentials in interreligious dialogue and a marked sensitivity for the constructive dimensions of the gospel. Yet he admitted to me that he would have stood up and walked out of church that morning after hearing the scripture readings if he had not feared offending the Catholic friends who had invited him. The strong implication that Jews were collectively responsible for the murder of the messiah, the deicide charge that has caused so much suffering and death for Jews throughout history, and John's talk of the disciples hiding for fear of "the Jews" were difficult words for this man who has always tried to combine a deep appreciation of his faith tradition with a genuine openness to Christianity.

On the basis of the readings he had heard, is it possible for the church to respect Judaism? Vatican Council II and statements by popes from John XXIII to John Paul II would seem to say yes. But he had to wonder what the congregants would believe in this regard. Matters were made even worse by the presider, who in the prayers of the faithful thanked God for the faith "the Jews could not have." Had the conciliar declaration on the Jews, *Nostra Aetate*, the 1975 Vatican guidelines and a series of guidelines from the American bishops made any impact? Or was the typical Catholic's attitude towards Jews and Judaism still shaped by the image of Jews as "rejectionists," and dangerous ones at that, rather than as a people whose faithfulness to the word of God remains unwavering? In the book, *The*

REV. DANIEL DUTKOFSKI

St Mary Parish
320 Middle Avenue
Elyria, Ohio 44035

323-5539

Cleveland Line 777-7380

Body of Faith, the ecumenical Jewish scholar Michael Wyschograd raises this question quite directly: "Why is it that Christians focus only on the moments of Israel's unfaithfulness and almost never at all on the moments of deep and uncompromising faithfulness?"

A Real Tension

We need to take my rabbinic friend's troubled reaction to one part of the Easter season very seriously in light of the call for increased Christian appreciation of Judaism and improved Christian-Jewish relations by Vatican Council II and recent popes. For this rabbi was in fact raising questions about attitudes which permeate the scripture selections in the three cycles of Easter readings — attitudes which have a pronounced anti-Judaic potential.

And this is the nub of the problem of conveying a positive sense of Judaism in liturgy, catechetics or theology. Anti-Judaic statements that are easily transformed into outright anti-Semitism are found at the core of the Christian proclamation. The problem will not be resolved simply by eliminating a few scripture passages or prayers from liturgical use. It always amazes me that people in the church think the dilemma of anti-Judaism and the scriptures is over and done with, that the problem was totally resolved by the council and the actions of Pope John XXIII when he struck the term "perfidious Jews" from the Good Friday liturgy. The readings of the Easter cycles and my rabbinic colleague's reaction to one part of them should convince otherwise.

What, then, are the principal sources of tension for the contemporary Christian-Jewish encounter arising out of the Eastertime Sunday readings? The first is the overriding impression that the Jews put Jesus to death because he was challenging the superficiality of their faith. On the Third Sunday of Easter in cycle A we hear Peter charge the "men of Israel" with using "pagans to crucify and kill" Jesus after he had proven himself as one sent by God. The tenor of the argument is much the same in the B cycle selection for the same Sunday. Peter bluntly blames the people (Jews by implication) for the failure of Pilate to release Jesus: "You disowned the Holy and Just One and preferred instead to be granted the release of a murderer. You put to death the author of life." Similar thoughts about Jewish responsiblity for the crucifixion occur on the Fourth Sunday of Easter (cycles A and B).

Understanding the Full Context

These texts easily reinforce an anti-Judaic interpretation of the Christian message. We should not pretend otherwise. Hence, these texts need to be met head-on by the homilist. Two points are crucial here for interpreting the church-synagogue relationship within the New Testament. The first is setting such statements within their original social context to the extent that contemporary scholarship can recreate that. The second is placing various New Testament texts dealing with the same subject matter side-by-side so that an overall assessment can be made of the thrust of an argument. In other words, when the New Testament exhibits differing emphases with respect to the same issue, no one text should be proclaimed to the congregation as the New Testament viewpoint.

Peter's statements in Acts of Jewish responsibility for the death of Jesus need to be subjected to the application of both principles. The social context is crucial. Peter is still speaking from within the larger Jewish community to people who look upon themselves as faithful Jews. The first reading from Acts 2, used in the A cycle for the Second Sunday of Easter, reports that the followers of Jesus "went to the Temple area together every day, while in their homes they broke bread."

So it seems that for Peter's Jerusalem community, the Jewish tradition remained vital to their faith expression despite their experience of a renewed vision in Jesus. Peter believed that what Jesus had given his disciples would enhance rather than obliterate the Torah that had provided meaning and direction for their lives. In sharing the enthusiasm for the new vision in Christ, Peter obviously became frustrated when the Jewish leadership and many of the people seemed unwilling to be touched by the joy and vitality the vision had added to the Jewish faith of the apostolic church. Frustration born out of enthusiasm for a new vision often leads to exaggerated charges. Some of that is likely operative in Acts. After weighing the evidence regarding Jewish responsibility for Jesus' death found in the relevant New Testament books, biblical scholars today have a strong consensus that at best a select number of Jewish leaders collaborated with the Roman imperial government in the decision to execute. And many of these Jewish leaders were not highly regarded within Jewish circles of the time and were looked upon as exploiters of their own people for personal gain.

What we have in Acts may be a case of youthful enthusiasm in the midst of identity development which led to the early Christian community's extension of blame beyond the actual facts of the case. It must also be said that it is not fully clear whom Peter is blaming in some of the passages. In certain cases the accusation seems to be directed against leaders, in others against the people-at-large. Nor can we discount the possibility that Peter's speeches reflect the spirit of competition for converts with Judaism and growing institutional estrangement that were prevalent at the time of the composition of Acts (70 CE or later). We may be dealing here with a reflection of the social context of the Jewish-Christian relationship in the latter part of the first century rather than with the actual attitudes of the post-Easter Jerusalem church.

Homilists and catechists will certainly want to convey the spirit and enthusiasm of the early church. But in so doing the responsibility to place Peter's remarks in their full context is part of the reconciliation between Jews and Christians to which we have been summoned by both John XXIII and John Paul II.

The Faithful Jews

A related concern which emerges from the Easter season readings is the depiction of Jews exclusively as obstructionists, nay-sayers, with respect to the gospel. The reading from John used each year on the Second Sunday of Easter and repeated every Pentecost describes the disciples hiding for fear of "the Jews." Without doubt this leaves a negative image with hearers of the word in our time. The same holds for the story of the dismissal of the apostles by the Sanhedrin and the order "not to speak again about the name of Jesus" from the selection from Acts for the Third Sunday of Easter (C cycle). See also the first reading for the Fourth Sunday of Easter (C cycle) which speaks of the expulsion of Paul and Barnabas from Antioch, and the Fifth Sunday (B cycle) which mentions the attack on Paul by the Greek-speaking Jews.

Again the social context becomes important in any interpretation of these texts. In John's gospel we come face-to-face with the thorny problem of his generalized use of "the Jews" rather than referring, as the other gospels do, to specific Jewish groups. This problem is not totally resolved in scholarly circles. And there may be no one alternative term applicable to the Johannine use of "the Jews." But in this selection it appears that the Jewish leadership, probably those connected with the temple administration, were the only ones intended.

As for the other passages, some of the points made earlier about the murder of the Messiah apply as well. Our sympathies as Christian worshipers will certainly remain in large measure with Paul and the apostles. Some of the people who opposed them were undoubtedly bent on safeguarding their own interests, but that is not the full story. As we Christians share anew each Easter season the vision of Christ proclaimed by the apostles, we must recognize that some of the Jewish leaders who opposed them may not have been mere obstructionists protecting their own flank. Rather, they may have been gravely concerned that the manner of proclamation and the decisions of the early church with respect to the place of the Jewish tradition might undermine the religious vision of the Hebrew Scriptures (which, we know, was central for Jesus himself). They may likewise have concluded that some of the enthusiastic announcements about the presence of the final kingdom may have been dangerously premature, despite a growing awareness of the imminence of the kingdom in rabbinic circles. In this area the church had to draw back somewhat by the end of the first century.

As we reflect on the significance of these passages today, two attitudes need to emerge. First is the clear recognition and proclamation that the Jewish "no" to Jesus may not simply have been hardheaded rejection but an attempt to preserve the religious roots of the gospel in the Jewish tradition (which the church has not done all that well over the centuries), and to warn us of the abuses associated with some christological affirmations, excessively individualistic interpretations of the Christ-event's significance for human salvation which have frequently crept into the church's spirituality and liturgy.

The second attitude is that conveyed in the remarkable paper presented by Professor Tomaso Federici, a Roman biblical scholar, at an international meeting of Catholics and Jews in 1978. In that paper Professor Federici argued that dialogue between Christians and Jews must now become the norm for carrying out the "witness" mandate of the risen Christ. In the dialogue we Christians will certainly wish in an appropriate manner to share the enthusiasm generated within us when hearing of the church's birth. But we will also recognize that in the struggle to establish its distinct identity in the separation of church and synagogue, Christianity may have seriously eroded, if not totally lost, a precious legacy—the tradition of the Hebrew Scriptures and the reflections upon them by subsequent generations of Jewish religious teachers. Such a wholesale discarding of the Jewish tradition was definitely not in the mind of Jesus as he proclaimed his message. It would have been impossible for Jesus to give us the word he did if he had not been able to draw upon the prophets and the Torah and the further developments in Judaism associated with the pharisaic revolution.

A gospel without its Jewish base is a truncated form of Jesus' message. This is what the Jewish "no" to Jesus, despite its awkwardness and its difficulty for the apostles at the time, has preserved for Christians today. Thus, in the dialogue, we Christians also need to encounter Jewish faith expressions. We do not enter the contemporary dialogue with Jews simply as "givers," but also as "receivers." This is a thrust that must be conveyed in proclaiming and teaching the word throughout the Easter season. In this regard it is unfortunate that the Hebrew Scriptures are not used at all during this season. For it leaves the impression that the Hebrew Scriptures have no part in the positive expression of the fundamentals of our faith as Christians. It blocks our ability to recognize, for example, that the reality of the Spirit that we proclaim so prominently during this season is a profoundly Jewish reality spoken of in the book of Joel and elsewhere.

Continuity with Jewish Roots

In concluding this examination of the anti-Semitic potential in the readings of the Easter season, mention needs to be made of the narrative of the Council of Jerusalem found in the Acts reading on the Sixth Sunday of Easter (C cycle). The results of the council—nonmaintenance of Jewish practices such as circumcision for new converts to the church—had a profound effect on Christianity's future orientation. Our impulse as Christians is to identify with Paul's defense of "freedom" on this question while looking upon the Jerusalem church led by Peter and James as unnecessarily restricted in its outlook. Perhaps the latter was such. But before we applaud Paul's victory at the council too loudly we ought at least consider the side of Peter and James. Though they, too, were concerned about the forging of a new identity for the young and growing church, they rightly believed that deep ties with the Jewish tradition should remain, for these were crucial for Jesus. They no doubt understood how profoundly the Jewish tradition had shaped his own thinking from their personal association with his ministry. To sever abruptly the church's Jewish roots risked seriously vitiating the gospel. Reluctantly they went along with Paul, concluding that circumcision and other Jewish practices were not the best way to accomplish this goal.

But Peter's and James' worst fears were frequently realized in subsequent centuries. Paul may have been right in setting Christianity on a new course. But Peter and James were also correct in insisting on the continuation of ties with the Jewish tradition. It is a shame that the epistle of James is not read in the Sunday liturgy during the Easter season (though it is used on weekdays and in the liturgy of the hours), for its thoroughly Jewish perspective can counteract the danger of a totally separatist mentality with respect to Judaism that can result from listening to the report of the Council of Jerusalem.

The Easter season is certainly a time of joy and vitality. The homilist and catechist need to make the Spirit come alive in reflections on the proclaimed word. But there is a need as well to remind Christians continually that the narrative of the young church's struggle for identity must be set in the context of the whole New Testament, including the pervasive Jewish spirit of Jesus' teachings as reported in the gospels and Paul's mature observations (Romans 9—11) about the ongoing validity of Judaism.

PART TWO

Notes for Homilists and Catechists

James A. Wilde

Whether in the pulpit, classroom discussion group, Bible study or sacramental preparation program, it does not take the homilist or catechist long to realize that a painful ignorance about Jewish people and Judaism still abounds. The Jew as devil, Christ killer, perpetually cursed usurer and penny-pinching cheat, the people whose faith was rejected and replaced by triumphant Christianity, the Jew whose holy book became the antithesis of love and the Spirit—anti-Semitic caricatures persist mightily.

Catechists, homilists and religious educators with their opportunity for presentation or dialogue over periods of time may have the most effective forum for clarifying issues on the Christian side of the Jewish-Christian relationship. To remedy the painful ignorance which Christians exhibit about Jews, Christian catechesis and preaching need to reflect Jewish people and Judaism accurately and honestly. To help accomplish this, the practical points which follow relate directly to the lectionary and Jewish-Christian relations.

1. *Rabbi Yeshua*

Jesus was Jewish to the core of his being. He was made "son of the covenant" by circumcision on the eighth day of his life. He probably spoke a Galilean dialect of Aramaic. He loved Torah and the traditions of his ancestors. And finally, not only were his friends Jewish but he was called "Rabbi" in the gospels.

"Christ" is not Jesus' last name. He was not addressed that way, nor was he addressed by the Hebrew word of which Christ is a Greek translation: Messiah. This title was given to him as the early church reflected on the meaning of his life and death, as we see in the gospels and other Christian writings.

2. *New Testament Affirms the Old*

Christian Scriptures build on and continue the Hebrew Scriptures. A hermeneutic of antithesis between the two is foreign to both. Both await the final fulfillment; both rest on love of God and neighbor (Deuteronomy 6:5; Leviticus 19:18; Matthew 22:34-40); and both find the beginnings of faith and election in the patriarchs, Moses and the prophets. A Christian who says that the Hebrew Bible is based on legalism and fear needs to study the facts and consider a change of attitude.

3. *Judaism at Jesus' Time Was Pluralistic*

In the first part of the first century, trends and sects within Judaism varied greatly. A movement toward orthodoxy was not evident until after the destruction of Jerusalem in 70 CE. Until that time, historical records (including the *Talmud*) disclose at least seven distinct classes of Pharisees with a great diversity of leadership styles. Judaism at that time embraced such variations in political, spiritual, religious, social and cultural values that generalizations are little more than meaningless.

For example, Rabbi Hillel, the leader of two pharisaic schools a little before Jesus' time, reflected in his teaching a marvelous balance of reason, gentleness and compassion for the poor. He taught:

If I am not for myself, who will be for me?
But when I am for myself alone, what good am I?
If not now, when?

Hillel was a pacifist and interpreted Torah in an integrated and pastoral way.

Be like the followers of Aaron, loving peace and pursuing it,
loving your fellow creatures.
What is hateful to you, do not do to your neighbor;
that is the whole Torah; the rest is commentary.

On the other hand, Rabbi Shammai, a contemporary of Hillel, had the reputation of being impatient and more attentive to details of Torah then to its integrated meaning. Several other rabbinic schools flourished in the first part of the first century, including that of Gamaliel I, Hillel's son and successor.

Zealots distinguished themselves from Pharisees like Hillel in their need physically to raise weapons against Rome. Even among the Zealots—from the Maccabees to Simon bar Kochba—diversity of lifestyle was great.

Essenes, unlike the Pharisees or Zealots, withdrew to wilderness communes like Qumran so they would not be negatively affected by the "inequities which became common among city dwellers" (*Manual of Discipline*). Ritual purification—in the form of initiatory water rites, prayers and hymns— was central for Essenes, along with a doctrine of the resurrection of the body, day of judgment, apocalyptic holy war and life in the world to come. Many of the Pharisees shared this doctrine.

Sadducees disagreed sharply with Pharisees and Essenes, however, by acknowledging only written Torah as authoritative. According to them, the oral tradition of rabbis and of communes like that of Qumran carried no weight. And since the doctrine of resurrection, judgment and life to come was part of that oral tradition, Sadducees were labeled as "those who do not believe in the resurrection." Upper class Jews connected with the priesthood of Zaddoq, the Sadducees were by far the most influential among all the landholders and merchants of the time. They may have posed a greater threat to Jesus, the Essenes and the Pharisees than has formerly been acknowledged. However, because their ranks were decimated and literature destroyed by the Romans in 70 CE, very little evidence remains to express their viewpoint.

Finally, Herodians distinguished themselves as promoters of Roman authority. Their pro-Roman stance made them opponents to Zealot movements most of all and also to many Pharisees.

Therefore, because of this diversity within Judaism at Jesus' time, it is unfair to generalize about Pharisees—much less, Jews—in any kind of derogatory way. Catechists need to be aware of this diversity and reflect it in discussions.

4. *How Did Jesus' Teaching Differ?*

It didn't differ a whole lot from the teaching of the Pharisees or Essenes. Historically, Jesus was part of a Second Temple period renewal effort within the larger Jewish community. His reverence for Torah and the prophets was shared by many other Jews in differing ways. Like most other rabbis of the time, he spoke against the impersonal legalism and routine ritual of some of the priestly leaders.

From a strictly historical perspective, insofar as we can know, Jesus' preaching and teaching distinguished itself from that of the majority of his fellow rabbis as follows:

- The arrival of the kingdom of God was seen as more imminent than many others thought. "If you see that it is by the finger of God that I cast out demons, then you know that the kingdom of God is upon you" (Luke 11:20). This statement was so characteristically and distinctly that of Jesus, even Rabbi Hillel could not agree with it completely. Jesus went further than others.

- Jesus ate with tax collectors and sinners, and of such was the messianic age he proclaimed. Each of the Jewish parties—like the rabbinic schools, the Essenes, the Zealots, the Sadducees—tried to enlist recruits into their ranks from among the vast body of disenfranchised, unattached "people of the land" (*am ha-aretz*). Jesus did the same by drawing closer to them than others did. His solidarity with them from a pharisaic perspective upset the apple cart of kingdom righteousness. Most Pharisees agreed that Torah admitted of variation in application, but Jesus pressed the variation further than they did.

- Love of enemies and forgiveness seven times seventy times are related themes peculiar to Jesus. Jesus carried pacifism further even than the Qumran community whose *Scroll of the War Between the Sons of Light and the Sons of Darkness* envisaged a kind of transposed or projected apocalyptic battle of good and evil rather than a here-and-now exhortation to love and forgive. Tolerance of enemies and peaceful coexistence with offenders is encouraged by several rabbis, but Jesus went further.

- The supererogatory deeds of love distinguish Jesus' teaching from others. "When a person strikes you on the right cheek, turn and offer him the other. When one asks for your shirt, give him your coat as well. If someone asks you to go a mile, go two"—is all material that is peculiar to Jesus.

- Though most of Jesus' teaching on kingdom righteousness seems to be against the legalism of Shammai and in support of the pastoral understanding of Hillel, the issue of divorce is a notable exception. Shammai interpreted Torah to allow divorce only in cases of proven adultery. Hillel interpreted Torah to allow divorce for several other reasons as well. It is historically highly probable that Jesus, on the other hand, interpreted Torah to allow no divorce under any circumstance. Whether the appeal to the authority of the account of creation in Mark 10:5ff. as the reason for this strong position was his own or that of a later editor is not clear.

- Jesus performed exorcisms. In Jesus' teaching, the relation between his exorcisms and the kingdom of God was close. Neither were unusual in themselves, but the connection between the two was peculiar to him. In the teaching of Jesus, exorcisms were a kind of object lesson for reflection on the nature of the kingdom, and this distinguished it from that of other rabbis.

This should suffice to paint a kind of shadow picture of how Jesus' teaching differed from that of most other rabbis. This part of the picture is, of course, incomplete. But what is even more grossly distorted by this kind of picture is the implication that the above characteristics also mark the heart of his teaching. They do not. The heart of his teaching about the kingdom of God is shared by most of the rabbis of his day (and our own): the messianic age is coming; prepare for it through repentance and the pursuit of righteousness before God, who is loving and merciful like a father.

Hillel died probably about five or ten years before Jesus was born. His son Gamaliel succeeded him as director of the Jerusalem rabbinic school which bore his name. And Paul the apostle, who stated, "I am a Jew, born at Tarsus, but brought up in this city [Jerusalem] at the feet of Gamaliel" (Acts 22:3; see Acts 26:4; Galatians 1:14), inherited through him the spirit of his father. How close Jesus got to Hillel's school is an open question. And how close Paul got to Yohanan ben Zakkai, Hillel's youngest and ultimately most influential student, is likewise unknown. It is interesting that the author of Acts paints Rabbi Gamaliel in much kinder colors than he does Rabbi Saul of Tarsus.

All of the above people were Jewish rabbis who held in common a deep love of God and Torah and the prophets. They differed to be sure. But this *intramural* nature of Christian beginnings within Judaism needs to be much more deeply appreciated by both Jews and Christians today.

5. *Who Killed Jesus?*

Several distinctions are needed. First, Jesus Christ underwent his passion and death *freely,* out of great love for his fellow human beings, that all might receive forgiveness of sin and reach salvation. It is entirely appropriate for this reason to lay the death of Jesus at the feet of every human being. Theologically therefore, with the Jewish historian Ellis Rivkin, the question is not *"Who* killed Jesus?" It is *"What* killed Jesus?" And the answer lies in the sin of every human being.

Second, historically Jesus was killed by *some* Jews and *some* Romans, but Christians have played up Jewish involvement and played down Roman involvement. This playing up and playing down continually needs to be held up to the light of historical criticism.

In the trial of Jesus, the role of Pontius Pilate, a Roman, may have been more than the "rubber stamp" that Mark, the other synoptics and John indicate at first glance. The striking discrepancies between the personality of Pilate in Mark and the personality of Pilate in the writings of Philo, Josephus and several others at least raise a question. Roman law gave Pilate total authority in a death penalty for political reasons like this one. Though we do not know of any evidence against Jesus, some members of the Roman Empire got rid of him, and some members of the Jewish Temple priesthood seemed to have a deep interest in the case. Moreover, it was Pilate who sentenced Jesus to death, a sentence his soldiers carried out in the Roman style of execution by crucifixion—not in the Jewish style of execution by stoning. Historically, Romans probably had more to do with the death of Jesus than the Christian Scriptures lead one to think. As historical documents, they are hardly neutral. The Christian Scriptures always favor Christians, and when they were being written it was dangerous to criticize Rome.

Third, Jews and Romans of today should not be held responsible for what some of their ancestors did. To hold them so is the height of prejudice and therefore completely at variance with Christian values.

6. *Judaism Lives Today*

As a religion, Judaism is just as valid, just as rich, and just as vital today as it ever was. The election and mission of Jewish people has permanent importance, and they play a decisive role in the religious history of humanity. Jewish history did not end with Jesus or the destruction of Jerusalem or the massive exterminations of this century. As Paul, a Jew, said, "Because of their fathers, this people remains most dear to God, for God does not repent of the gifts he makes nor of the calls he issues" (Romans 11:28f.).

As Christians we believe that the tradition of Israel was opened by the coming of Jesus Christ to the whole gentile world. Nevertheless, as Christians we do not devalue the renaissance of Judaism which took place in the centuries immediately following the time of Jesus, nor, for that matter, do we discount in any way the whole subsequent history of Judaism, including that of our own day.

7. *Jewish People Related to the Land of Israel*

Without adopting a political stance in the present controversies in the Middle East, the catechist affirms the religious attachment between the Jewish people and the Land of Israel (*eretz Israel*) as one that finds its roots in biblical tradition and is central to Jewish covenant faithfulness to the one God. The Roman Catholic tradition affirms the existence of the State of Israel on the basis of the common principles of international law.

At the same time, a catechist in the Roman Catholic tradition must avoid the approach of biblical fundamentalism which tends to interpret current political events in the Middle East in an allegorical way. This means that for a lectionary discussion group or Bible study class to speculate on the end of the world in view of political options in the eastern Mediterranean, for example, is a foolish waste of time. Further, such speculation trivializes the important issues of biblical faith both for Jews and for Christians.

8. *How Did the Jewish-Christian Divorce Come About?*

No one knows for sure. Evidence from both sides and from neutral sources points to the decade immediately following the destruction of Jerusalem in 70 CE as the critical one. For Paul the apostle and for the author of the Gospel of Mark, it seems, the relationship between Jews and Christians was still an intramural one, as we discussed above. But in the Gospel of Matthew, written later, the social boundaries of Christianity vis-a-vis Judaism were hardening. The language used against Judaism in the Gospel of Matthew (and Luke and John) is more bitter and even abusive than in the Gospel of Mark (compare, for example, Mark 12:38-40 with Matthew 23:1-38). Apparently Paul and the author of the earliest gospel both hoped for a kind of "Israel of the Nations" (certainly not like the contemporary syncretistic movements variously called "messianic Jews" or "Jews for Jesus," some members of whom have openly devalued the validity both of contemporary Judaism and contemporary Christianity and proselytized from both), but the author of the Gospel of Matthew realized it was not going to happen in his lifetime.

From the Jewish side, Rabbi Yohanan ben Zakkai's departure from Jerusalem after its destruction and his establishment of Yavneh (Jamnia) as the post-Jerusalem center of Judaism marks a significant turning point. Curiously this transfer of power within Judaism was probably what ultimately alienated "non-orthodox" (by Zakkai's standards, heretical) people like the author of the Gospel of Matthew. Why? Because along with the geographical and power shift from Jerusalem to Yavneh came an even more important spiritual and political change.

The great renaissance of Torah under Yohanan ben Zakkai at Yavneh brought with it a political stance over against Rome which led to the end of pluralistic or sectarian Judaism (which included even gentile converts) and the birth of "official" Judaism. The leadership at Yavneh rejected any association with the military ways of the by then decimated but still threatening rebel Zealots in order to remain above suspicion by Rome. Unfortunately this led them also to reject association with another group of Jews and gentiles who claimed to be followers of a messiah. Fearing that Rome would not make the fine distinctions between pacifist messiah followers, which included gentiles, and strictly Jewish Zealot messiah followers in the heat of war, Zakkai and other leaders at Yavneh drew a line. They chose a less dangerous route.

Therefore, after 70 CE, for reasons of political survival and injured pride, Jews and Christians went their separate ways—the saddest chapter in their history. The children with a common ancestry in Abraham parted. Has misunderstanding ever been so costly to either side?

9. *The Language of Jewish-Christian Unity*

Words can be two-edged swords. Images run close to attitudes. The language of distance and prejudice cannot be confused with the language of unity. Therefore use of some new words and images in liturgical and catechetical situations could help the Jewish-Christian cause. We have already used the image of children with a common ancestry to describe the relationship between Jews and Christians.

Catechists and preachers might well speak of the relation between the Hebrew and Christian Scriptures not as "shadow" and "reality" but as "foundation" and "building." Care should be taken so that "old" is not understood as "out of date" or "outworn." The Old Testament (Hebrew

Scriptures) has permanent value as a source of revelation (see the Vatican II *Declaration of the Relation of the Church to Non-Christian Religions*, #4, and the *Dogmatic Constitution on Divine Revelation*, #3) for Jews and for Christians.

One of the most helpful images is still that of the root and the branches in Romans 11:17-24:

> If some of the branches were cut off and you, a branch of the wild olive tree, have been grafted in among the others and have come to share in the rich root of the olive, do not boast against the branches. If you do boast, remember that you do not support the root; the root supports you. You will say, "Branches were cut off that I might be grafted in." Well and good. They were cut off because of unbelief and you are there because of faith. Do not be haughty on that account, but fearful. If God did not spare the natural branches, he will certainly not spare you.
>
> Consider the kindness and the severity of God—severity toward those who fell, kindness toward you, provided you remain in his kindness; if you do not, you too will be cut off. And if the Jews do not remain in their unbelief they will be grafted back on, for God is able to do this. If you were cut off from the natural wild olive and, contrary to nature, were grafted into the cultivated olive, so much the more will they who belong to it by nature be grafted into their own olive tree.

The dominant theme is that the Israel of Abraham, Isaac, Jacob, Moses and the prophets is the root of the olive tree. The branches are Paul's contemporary Christians and Jews, united both at their source and in their intertwining.

Paul's evaluation of the faith of his fellow Jews, even though they, God's own people, rejected God's own son as well as God's own gospel, is ultimately positive. In his agonized but conscientious wrestling with the divine plan on this issue, he concludes, in verses 28f. of the same chapter:

> In respect to the gospel, the Jews are enemies of God for your sake; in respect to the election, they are beloved by him because of the patriarchs. God's gifts and his call are irrevocable.

In Ephesians 2:11-13, the image of "city" and "citizenship" to describe the relation between Jews and Christians is implied as follows:

> You men of Gentile stock, remember that in former times you had no part in Christ and were excluded from the community of Israel. You were strangers to the covenant and its promise; you were without hope and without God in the world. But now in Christ Jesus you who once were far off have been brought near through the blood of Christ.

Likewise in Matthew 8:11, the church is described as a guest entering the city to "find a place at the banquet in the kingdom of God with Abraham, Isaac and Jacob." Christians therefore become citizens in the city of Israel.

All these words evoke images of complementarity and wholeness, and sometimes it is the words themselves that can accomplish more than logical argument to paint the desired picture. We recommend careful use of them.

10. *Holocaust*

In a discussion that touches on the extermination of the massive numbers of Jews at the hands of the National Socialist Party of Germany between 1939 and 1945, two things are required of the catechist, and both are challenging.

First, the underlying issues need to be brought into focus in the catechist's mind. The stock questions continually arise: Could it happen again? And a stock answer is: Yes, of course. And it does. Or questions may arise about the numbers, the places, the particular methods and the lives of escapees. However, as important as these facts of the extermination are, they can distract from the central issues. One of the central issues, this writer submits, is that the holocaust is not a Jewish-Nazi matter. It is a human one. It is as broad and deep as humanity itself.

Ultimately the real issue becomes a personal one for every Christian who thinks about the Jewish massacres in Europe— or any form of anti-Semitic abuse, past and current. The personal questions for that Christian become: "What does this have to do with me? And God? Am I willing to meet God face to face over this matter? Am I willing to face the truest reality in all things, the very first, center and very last? Can I accept my own human life and my mortality? Am I in solidarity with my fellow suffering human beings who accept the truth of their mortal existence and who offer love and compassion? Or am I on the side of human beings who try to deny the truth of mortal existence by causing misery for others in a futile effort to rise above them for a moment of some kind of power and glory?" It is not unlike the questions, "Will I hurt this person for my own gain? Which do I want more for myself—a career of meaning and service or a quick buck?"

Second, the catechist needs to reframe the holocaust picture in the mind of each member of the discussion group or class in such a way that everyone becomes part of that picture. "The holocaust is my issue." Whether the members of the group are third graders or adults, the catechist's job is the same. Through storytelling and questions appropriate to the group, the catechist wants to provide insight which elicits a decision for or against a change of attitude—conversion. Conversion is the goal of preaching and catechizing. In the Bible, it means "changing one's mind" about something. So in this context, conversion means reframing the holocaust picture to include oneself.

Since this conversion is about faith, the stories one uses to elicit it really become parables of the kingdom of God. Superficially their content may have nothing to do with concentration camps, but they always underline the values we learn from the concentration camps in such dramatic ways— the values of the kingdom—like love of God and neighbor, the dignity of human life, justice, freedom, solidarity in suffering, silence, celebration, humor, hope and joy. Creative retelling of the classic stories of the Bible, telling one's own story in word or action and telling the stories of others— like the stories of the faith of holocaust victims and survivors—these can help set the stage for reaching the important goal of conversion.

11. *Expecting the Messianic Age*

The majority of Jews and Christians throughout history and today look forward with hope to a time of fulfillment, justice and new life. How that kingdom will come, when it will come, who will usher it in, exactly what it will be like, as well as the precise amount of human or divine agency required to bring it about—all these questions are answered with as much diversity within Judaism as they are within Christianity.

Christians speak of the first and second coming. They describe Jesus Christ as the "firstborn" of the new creation. Words like "guarantee," "prolepsis," or "proof" are used to talk about the relation between Jesus Christ's presence now in mystery and the final coming in glory.

Jews have a slightly simpler terminology. They look forward to the coming. Some expect a personal messiah. Others a messianic age. Some relate this messianic age to Zionism in various ways. One contemporary Jew, Elie Wiesel, a survivor of Auschwitz and the 1986 Nobel Peace Prize laureate, muses that the messianic age may be introduced by an anonymous beggar. Whereas, Rabbi Leon Klenicki, Director of the Interfaith Affairs Department of the Anti-Defamation League of B'nai B'rith, muses that it will be a woman.

Both Jews and Christians pray to the Father in hope for the coming of the kingdom in fullness. Both work to promote peace and justice in the world. In the words of the 1985 Vatican *Notes,* "Our aim should be to show the unity of biblical revelation (OT and NT) and of the divine plan, before speaking of each historical event, so as to stress that particular events have meaning when seen in history as a whole—from creation to fulfillment.''

12. *Catechetical Resources*

The entire Bible and the Bible in lectionary form are first on the list of catechetical resources. This writer recommends that catechists become totally familiar with the Bible. It calls for ongoing, lifelong study, meditation and prayer. Jews and Christians both believe it is God's word.

Second, the 1985 *Notes on the Correct Way to Present the Jews and Judaism in Preaching and Teaching in the Roman Catholic Church* by the Vatican Commission for Religious Relations with the Jews is necessary reading. It is a very helpful document.

Other recommended resources include the titles listed in the Selected Bibliography at the end of this book, especially the review *SIDIC*, published by the International Jewish-Christian Documentation Service, and *Face to Face: An Interreligious Bulletin*, published quarterly by the Anti-Defamation League of B'nai B'rith. On the matter of what Jesus was like and what he taught, the reader would do well to go to *The Quest of the Historical Jesus* by Albert Schweitzer (an older but classic treatment of how prejudices and presuppositions have determined different views of Jesus) or *Rediscovering the Teaching of Jesus* by Norman Perrin (a demonstration of how one determines the profile of Jesus' teaching with standard historical/literary critical tools).

For information on first-century Judaism, read any of the works of Jacob Neusner, expecially *First Century Judaism in Crisis* or *A Life of Yohanan ben Zakkai: Ca. 1-80 CE*. A classic and handy overview of the issues is *This Immortal People: A Short History of the Jewish People* by Emil Cohn, translated, revised and expanded by Hayim Perelmuter. See the Selected Bibliography for details.

PART THREE

Samples of How Catholics Speak about Jews

The following section includes:

- Homilies
- General Intercessions
- Reflections and Illustrations
- Bulletin Items

The following samples may be used as catalysts for speaking responsibly about Jews. The dating and lectionary information on some materials indicates in what connection they have been used. But it should not limit free adaptation. In fact, these samples serve best when they spark creativity, when they encourage one to "go and do likewise."

Sample Homilies

Epiphany
A Light of Revelation to the Gentiles

Isaiah 60:1-6

Ephesians 3:2-3, 5-6

Matthew 2: 2-12

The final chapters of Isaiah, 56 through 66, are the work of a lyrical poet who wishes to celebrate the marvels he has witnessed as the exiles, returned from Babylon, have set about rebuilding Jerusalem.

In the Soviet Union and countries within its orbit, statuary of heroic proportions rises in the public squares. You see farmers, factory workers, artisans of both sexes with shirts open, muscles gleaming, hammers held aloft and sickles arcing downward—a hymn in three dimensions to the power of human labor.

In Israel you see posters in tribute to the Zionist achievement all over the country. Depicted are young *kibbutzniks* who still exist in numbers but are no longer at the heart of the country's economy as they were in the founding days. Zionism is an achievement of the Jewish people who created it, and the founders are well remembered in the poetry, the songs and other mythology of that infant state.

The third Isaiah was an anonymous genius who attributed the marvel of rebuilding that was unfolding before his eyes to the God of Israel alone. Non-Jews could join themselves to the Lord in this work of restoration— even that once-proscribed, sexually powerless Jewish class, called the eunuchs—so long as the sabbath was not profaned in Jerusalem and the covenant was held to. There was much immoral behavior abroad among the sons and daughters of Judah in those days of return from exile: sorcery, infant sacrifice, heavy drinking, corruption and profiteering. The poet in chapters 57, 58 and 59 sounds as if he were describing the Old West or the Klondike in the gold rush.

Your fast ends in quarreling and fighting, striking with vicious blow . . .

Is this the kind of fasting I look for . . .

Do you call this . . . a day acceptable to the Lord? . . .

This, rather, is the fasting that I wish:

Release those bound unjustly . . . Share your bread with the hungry . . .

Shelter the oppressed and the homeless . . . Clothe the naked when you
see them, not turning your back on your own. (Isaiah 58:4-7)

The poet in spelling out the side effects of economic recovery has a lively sense of human responsibility—there is no doubt of it. But when chapter 60 is reached, which is our first reading, the marvel of Zion's renewal is to be attributed solely to its God. The earth is in darkness and clouds cover the people but its light is the glory of the Lord. When the riches of the seas are emptied out and the wealth of nations is brought to Zion, it will be no economic miracle of postwar recovery. It will be the Lord's doing: dromedaries from Midian and Ephah, all from Sheba bearing gold and frankincense, five-tiered oarsmen of Nineveh bringing ivory, apes and peacocks.

Poor poets of old, how little they knew of the balance of trade! They thought that the earth was the Lord's, that the heathen could not *but* come suppliant to Holy Zion because the Israel of the future would be sons and daughters of light, refracting the splendor of their God.

Once you were forsaken, hated and unvisited,

Now I will make you the pride of the ages . . .

You shall suck the milk of nations and be nursed at royal breasts.

You shall know that I the Lord am your Savior, the Mighty One of
Jacob your redeemer . . . (60:15-16)

We celebrate today the manifestation of a God of light, whose fitting symbol is a guiding star, to a non-Jewish world—which is most of the world of learning. The intellectuals of the East with their arcane knowledge of the skies are taken into the camp of the God of Israel by Matthew, just as the heathen traders had been co-opted by the third Isaiah. This feast of *Showing God's Glory Forth* has in the past featured other manifestations, chiefly that of Jesus at the Jordan at his baptism and the first of his signs at Cana in Galilee. But the disclosure of God's long-harbored secret to put gentiles on an even footing with Jews, made to the gentiles through the Magi, has won the day literally: the liturgical day.

We—the far greater number of us—are "the gentiles." Our joyous claim is that in Christ Jesus we are now co-heirs with the Jews, members of the same body, sharers of the promise through the preaching of the gospel. The Jews never invited us into their company on these terms, but then they never asked to be a people set apart, a chosen race, a royal priesthood in the first place. We need to walk very warily here. What Jews do and say about their chosenness is a matter between them and their covenant God. It is our business to affirm their covenant status as the very condition of our acknowledging a secret within godhead concerning us. We say, "the mystery has been disclosed to us." We must do more. We must harbor our election as a treasure of grace, preaching to non-Jews like ourselves the unfathomable riches of Christ, of which the chief is the religion of Israel.

In Christ Jesus, the censures of the ancient prophet lie even heavier upon us than before. "I will appoint peace your governor and justice your ruler," said the Lord. The name Christian as a cloak for our greed, our prejudice, our pursuit of the arts of war, is Christ besmirched, the gospel betrayed, our call as gentiles mocked.

We turn back then, to the work of praise in which we are engaged—one with Israel if, as a worshiping people they will have us—humbled by the call to enlighten all regarding God's mysterious design. It is a call to liberate, to enlarge, to affirm all that is human. Oh, what an epiphany *that* would be!

Gerard S. Sloyan

Good Friday
Is the Cross a Sword of Division?

Isaiah 52:13-53:12

Hebrews 4:14-16 5:7-9

John 18:1-19, 42

Today's liturgy confronts us in a special way as Christian believers with the reality of the cross. Death, desolation, separation, exile, sin are all part of that reality as we learn from the readings, the music and the prevailing mood of the day.

The church calls us to strip ourselves bare for a moment, to shed the ordinary masks that so often hide the continuing presence of sin in our lives and deflect us from genuine encounter with the forces of death and destruction around us. Yet a note of hope and triumph remain for us. While darkness abounds, it is not ultimately the dominant reality.

The reality that stands starkly before us on Good Friday in a way it does on no other day of the liturgical year is in the end only a rite of passage like death. This is the certainty of our Christian faith born out of the incarnation and resurrection. As difficult, as challenging as the Good Friday liturgy with its focus on the cross can be for sensitive Christians who participate in it with full intensity, in the end it strikes a positive chord.

Not so, my brothers and sisters, with some others who likewise share in our covenant faith. I speak of the Jewish community. For many of them the cross has become a symbol of alienation.

Father Edward Flannery, one of the American Catholic pioneers in Christian-Jewish reconciliation, describes this sense of Jewish apprehension in the introduction to his classic book on anti-Semitism, *The Anguish of the Jews*. The genesis of the volume, he tells us, goes back to an experience he had in the streets of New York one Christmas season while in the company of Jewish friends. They chanced upon a skyscraper with a huge illuminated cross upon it. Glancing over her shoulder, one of his friends, ordinarily well-disposed towards Christians, suddenly declared: "That cross makes me shudder. It is like an evil presence." Flannery was profoundly moved by her spontaneous reaction. He was forced to ask himself, as he says, "How did the cross, the supreme symbol of universal love, become a sign of fear, of evil for this young Jewess?"

Father Flannery's question is one we need to reflect on in a special way ourselves this Good Friday. Recent Catholic teachings, including strong statements from Pope John Paul II, have challenged every Catholic to re-examine how Jesus' profoundly Jewish doctrine of love and fundamental human respect to which he remained unalterably committed—even to the ultimate sacrifice of his life which we commemorate in this liturgy—became perverted into what has been called the "teaching of contempt." As a result of this Christian anti-Semitic teaching, millions of Jews were persecuted and even put to death at the hands of baptized people. It is a legacy we must painfully acknowledge as a Christian community.

Pope John Paul II, in a 1982 address at the Vatican, urged us to put aside this legacy of "misunderstandings, errors and insults" towards the Jewish community. There is need, he insisted, for us to overcome the past through a new emphasis on understanding, peace and mutual esteem. "The terrible persecutions suffered by the Jews in various periods of history," he said, "have finally opened many eyes and disturbed many hearts. Thus Christians are on the right path, that of justice and brotherhood, when they seek, with respect and perseverance, to gather with their Semitic brethren around the common heritage which is a treasure to us all."

What better time for each of us to begin this conversion, this reconciliation, than in this time of passover from darkness to light! This is a process that must involve each one of us. It is a task not only for the church's leadership and teachers. Christians everywhere must begin to see the cross of Good Friday as a mark of deep bonding between themselves and the Jewish people rather than as a sword of division as we have for so long a time.

This is not impossible. The prominent Lutheran theologian, Franklin Sherman, calls us to the reality of the cross as the symbol of an agonizing

God. He says, "It is tragic that this symbol should have become a symbol of division between Jews and Christians, for the reality to which it points is a Jewish reality as well, the reality of suffering and martyrdom."

John's account of the passion which we have heard today must be integrated into the history of Jewish suffering and martyrdom. What brought Jesus to his passion and death were traditional Jewish biblical values, strongly espoused by the prophets, which were being given new force and meaning at that time by the Pharisees with whom, as the recent Vatican *Notes* on Judaism tell us, Jesus shared so much in common. So often in the lenten season and especially during this sacred week, Christians have asked themselves who put Jesus to death. And so often they have wrongly and tragically answered, "the Jews. Even the author of the gospel just read answered this way." Though many may have gone on to add that the Romans were responsible as well, the Jewish community of the period were still considered the concrete historical agents of his death.

My friends, that can no longer be our main question. It must be replaced with the question, "*What* crucified Jesus?" What crucified Jesus was domination, tyranny, power and disregard for life. Such domination, such disregard for life was always opposed by the Jewish tradition. For example, in Jesus' time, it was the tyranny of the Romans who were in league with certain corrupt elements of the Jewish high priestly class. These collaborating priests were despised by most of the Jews of the time. Jesus' stance was unique in a number of crucial areas of religious teaching, but his criticism of the spiritual/political leadership of his time was shared by many of his Jewish brothers and sisters. It was this criticism which brought him to death on Calvary.

Imagine again what happened. See a picture in which Jesus stands not as an isolated prophet over against the entirety of the Jewish community of the time, but as a person within the progressive movements in Judaism. Along with the Pharisees he put himself against the Roman authorities and that small group of collaborationist Jews associated with them. The passion narrative of John, more than any of the others, makes the point quite strongly that the Romans rather than the Jews arrested Jesus, conducted his decisive trial and sentenced him to die for actions they considered "political crimes." These were actions Jesus saw as fundamental to the love and human dignity at the center of Jewish Torah—and this he never repudiated. Until we recapture this authentic spirit of Good Friday, our yearly commemoration of it will retain the potential for anti-Semitism.

This legacy of anti-Semitism, flowing from a false theology of the cross, has been a sword striking deeply against Jews. It has struck the Christian church as well. For it has tended to cut us off from a profoundly enriching source of Jesus' own spirituality—his Jewish roots. May those roots begin to grow in us again this Good Friday as we reflect on the martyrdom of our Jewish brother Jesus—and on the martyrdom of Jewish people throughout history.

John T. Pawlikowski

Third Sunday of Easter, cycle A
The Hard Struggle of Resurrection Faith

Acts 2:14, 22-28

1 Peter 1:17-21

Luke 24:13-35

The essential mysteries of the life of Christ—the mysteries of our faith—are learned anew each year and celebrated as prolonged seasons rather than a single day. Incarnation, suffering and death and finally resurrection are too rich to be perceived all at once.

Similarly, who of us can presume to be fully rational human beings on our seventh birthday, prepared to face the world on the day of high school graduation, mature at 21, and be ready for the perfect marriage on our wedding day? The mysteries of life and faith require reflection and acceptance. Christian life is not as simple as baptism, confirmation and eucharist. Grasping the mystery of Easter is not easy. That is why we have an entire season for discernment. We discover that our faith is not so sure. If we really confront the message of resurrection, we find ourselves at times no less incredulous than the disciples en route to Emmaus.

On that journey, only a short time after the most profound mystery of Christianity had occurred, we find the two saying to their unrecognized guest, with an air of resignation: "We were hoping that he was the one who would set Israel free." How confused those disciples were! They were even disappointed over the empty tomb. How deficient was their comprehension of the Easter event! They forgot the very basis for Christian hope, the resurrection.

To begin, we must keep in mind what the best biblical scholarship has discovered, that the Acts of the Apostles is probably a sequel to the Gospel of Luke and written by the same person. Both are written for non-Jewish audiences. And this in itself suggests a nuanced view about the Jews that is more hyperbole than reality. The image of the Jews presented in Acts is of a hopeless throng used as the vile instruments of God's reluctant plan for salvation. Hardly objective history! To cast all Jews in this mold is not only unfair but outrageous to the modern mind. Today's reading from Acts says, "He was delivered up by the set purpose and plan of God; you (Jews) even used pagans to crucify and kill him." Elsewhere the Jews are accused of killing "the author of life."

We must understand these difficult scriptural passages in context. First, the treasures of the Bible should never be limited to their face value. This is always a danger, to assume that what scriptures say is all that needs to be known. The late Rabbi Abraham Heschel said it well: "We attempt to confine God and the Bible to historical fact." We look upon it at times as a mass of enigmatic detail and lose the spirit. But he also said, "The Bible is an answer to the supreme question: What does God demand of us?" Though Heschel's references were to the Hebrew Scriptures, we may apply his words to our Christian Scriptures as well. The negative cast of the Jewish community as found in the Acts of the Apostles should not be accepted at face value. These words pose a real problem for Christians. Christians are the ones without hope if they do not believe in the resurrection. Here in the gospel passage, Christians are reprimanded for being "slow to believe."

The impatience of Jesus with the disciples on the road to Emmaus, the strong address of Peter at Pentecost ("for it was impossible that death should keep its hold on Jesus"), and the stern warning by the same apostle in one of the biblical letters ascribed to him, namely, that Christians "conduct themselves reverently" and keep their faith and hope "centered on God"—all these things reveal a problem Christians were having in accepting the Easter mystery. Why vilify the Jewish community then? It was not their problem.

In part we have here what modern day psychologists would call projection: the tendency to attribute to others those traits we dislike in ourselves. Added to this, Dr. Frederick Perls says, "is a certain kind of sympathy in which one feels oneself into the other person and solves one's own problems by solving his." Acknowledging a certain lack of faith in Christ's resurrection and disliking that weakness, the author of Acts may be said to have put on the Jews what is lacking in the Christians themselves.

Alternatively, the disassociation with mainstream Judaism could be considered an attempt by the early church to find its own identity. Our experience of daily life illustrates this activity vividly. We know that adolescence is a time for self-discovery and solidifying identity. The troublesome time of the teenage years is attributable in large part to the act of breaking away from the nest of one's parents. Unfortunately in this process, unfair and even hurtful things may be said, which of course are not true. Young people may cast their parents in less than positive roles. It is but the difficulty of growing up. In coming to grips with its new identity, the nascent church treated parent Judaism the same way.

Peter's letter to gentile Christians of Asia Minor, our modern day Turkey, makes the same point. "Your parents handed you a futile way of life." This sharp division between parent and offspring helps children establish a new identity, different from their parents. In our case, Peter is helping to establish a new identity among the Christians of gentile origin in that place at that time.

All three readings today were originally written for gentile audiences. Creating a strong group identity for the early Christians to whom they were addressed by portraying the Jewish community negatively played right into already existing prejudices. We can hardly call it coincidence.

But what then is revealed for us today in these readings? To be aware of our own struggles in accepting a very hard truth: Christ is risen from the dead. To be aware of the not so Christian ways we blame this frustration on others. Perhaps in our own life we chide others who do not share our religious identity or those whose level of religious or moral behavior seems opposite ours. We must keep in mind that believing is always a struggle. Frequently it takes a lifetime. Recall that it was during the ritual breaking of bread that the two disciples recognized Jesus. Each Sunday we are asked to break bread again to open our eyes that have been so frequently closed to previous revelations. The weekly celebration of Mass on Sunday—a little Easter—is a continually new revelation of a mystery hard to live.

Too often our impatience with ourselves spills over into projections of character and prejudice. Examined rationally we cannot denigrate the beliefs of others as though they were doing us harm. If anything we walk together in our common human paradox of dealing with things divine. Again the words of Rabbi Heschel tell us exactly how we should view these and all scriptures—not as bare facts but rather as a personal question, an ultimate question: "What does God demand of us?"

The names we call people of other faiths, particularly Jews, are unfair projections of our own lack of faith. Certainly charity never allows us to make accusations which have no substance and which come from our own fear. Scripture reveals something about us. This is how we best interpret it. When faced with difficult passages which create divisions and stir unwarranted feelings of animosity, we should place ourselves as the authors of such unfair attacks and ask why. It is then that we discover our real weakness. From this point we may begin to believe in Easter, by acknowledging that it is indeed a difficult mystery and only with the grace of God can we believe.

Robert B. Sherman

First Sunday of Advent, cycle A

That with our brothers and sisters of Zion, we beat swords into plowshares and spears into pruning hooks for the coming of the kingdom, we pray:

Second Sunday of Advent, cycle A

That Jews and Christians let the little child guide them as the kingdom comes with peace, we pray:

Third Sunday of Advent, cycle A

That all whom the Lord has ransomed—Jew and Christian alike—will enter Zion singing, crowned with lasting joy, we pray:

Fourth Sunday of Advent, cycle A

For all the children of David—Jews and Christians together—that we discover Emmanuel, we pray:

First Sunday of Advent, cycle B

That Jews and gentiles forgive each other and work together for the coming of the kingdom, we pray:

Second Sunday of Advent, cycle B

That Christians speak tenderly to Jerusalem as the Lord does, we pray:

Third Sunday of Advent, cycle B

That all of us anointed by the Spirit, Jew and Christian alike, bring glad tidings to the lowly as the Lord comes in glory, we pray:

Fourth Sunday of Advent, cycle B

That the people of Israel and the people of the church stand firm forever, we pray:

First Sunday of Advent, cycle C

That the house of Israel and the house of the church be safe as the Lord comes, we pray:

Second Sunday of Advent, cycle C

For our Jewish brothers and sisters, that they forgive us and work with us to prepare the way, we pray:

Third Sunday of Advent, cycle C

That the people of Israel and the people of the church rejoice with gladness as the Lord's reign comes near, we pray:

Fourth Sunday of Advent, cycle C

That God's flock be gathered from the ends of the earth, Jew and Christian alike, and come home together, we pray:

Epiphany, cycles A, B, C

That all nations come home to Jerusalem, the city of peace, we pray:

That the star lead us speedily to Jerusalem, that we may worship God in God's holy city, we pray:

That God who makes peace in high heaven will send this peace here below in our own day, to us and to our children, we pray:

First Sunday of Lent, cycle A

That we resist all temptation to prejudice, that we treat Jews, blacks, women and all human beings as God's children, we pray:

Second Sunday of Lent, cycle A

That God reveal the awesome glory today in church, synagogue, temple, and mosque just as from the cloudy mountain, we pray:

Third Sunday of Lent, cycle A

That Jews and gentiles, male and female, rich and poor, learn to live together in peace, we pray:

Fourth Sunday of Lent, cycle A

For our Jewish brothers and sisters whom we have wronged, that we and they know the oneness all people share in God, we pray:

Fifth Sunday of Lent, cycle A

That the people of Israel and the people of the church rise from their graves and rest in God, we pray:

Passion (Palm) Sunday, cycle A

That we receive pardon from God for beating the backs of the Jews for so long, we pray:

Good Friday, cycles A, B, C

Pastoral Note: The sixth petition of the General Intercessions in the Sacramentary for Good Friday is excellent as a prayer for the Jewish people, the first to hear the word of God. It needs no explanation.

The Reproaches, however, are optional and, if used, need careful explanation. One way to explain them beforehand is:

During the Reproaches that follow, we Christians must again personally place ourselves within the passion drama. For *we* led Christ to the cross. *We* yielded to bitterness. *We* offered him vinegar.

Easter Sunday, cycle A

That all of us whom God called through the waters, Jew and Christian alike, will never die again, we pray:

Second Sunday of Easter, cycle A

For Christians as they observe Easter and Pentecost, for Jews as they observe Passover and the Feast of Weeks, that we all come to know God's peace, we pray:

Third Sunday of Easter, cycle A

That we receive God's forgiveness for calling Jewish people Christ-killers for 1900 years, we pray:

Fourth Sunday of Easter, cycle A

That Jewish people pardon us Christians for blaming Christ's death on them, we pray:

Fifth Sunday of Easter, cycle A

That Jews and Christians work together to spread the word of God's love, we pray:

Sixth Sunday of Easter, cycle A

For the victims of prejudice—Jews, blacks and all the rest—that they come to know the true justice of God, we pray:

Seventh Sunday of Easter, cycle A

That the people of Israel receive God's blessing for giving us Jesus, his mother and all his friends, we pray:

Pentecost, cycle A

For all Christians and Jews, that they fear each other no longer, we pray:

First Sunday of Lent, cycle B

That all of us, Jew and Christian alike, proclaim God's good news in this time of fulfillment, we pray:

Second Sunday of Lent, cycle B

That the promises God made to Abraham and his seed be a blessing of peace for all the nations of the earth, we pray:

Third Sunday of Lent, cycle B

That zeal for God's house set hearts on fire in every church, synagogue and temple in the land, we pray:

Fourth Sunday of Lent, cycle B

That all Jews and gentiles scattered in the world come home to rest together, we pray:

Fifth Sunday of Lent, cycle B

That the children of God's covenant, Jew and Christian alike, receive the law in our hearts, we pray:

Passion (Palm) Sunday, cycle B

That all anti-Semitism be erased from the world, we pray:

Good Friday, cycle B
(See Good Friday, cycle A)

Easter Sunday, cycle B

As Jesus Christ rises in Jerusalem on Easter morning, may God draw all faithful Christians and faithful Jews to the heavenly Jerusalem in the kingdom, we pray:

Second Sunday of Easter, cycle B

For all who obey God's commandments, both Christian and Jew, that we work together with one heart and mind to serve the needy, we pray:

Third Sunday of Easter, cycle B

That we receive pardon from the God of Abraham, Isaac and Jacob for accusing Jews of killing the author of life, we pray:

Fourth Sunday of Easter, cycle B

For the people of Israel, that fullness of redemption be theirs forever, we pray:

Fifth Sunday of Easter, cycle B

That the wandering people of God, Christian and Jew alike, learn to care for each other, we pray:

Sixth Sunday of Easter, cycle B

That the children of Israel and the children of the church love one another as God loves us, we pray:

Seventh Sunday of Easter, cycle B

That the Hebrew and Christian Scriptures reach their fulfillment in the kingdom of God, we pray:

Pentecost, cycle B

That all the children of the covenant, the faithful of Israel and the faithful of the church, receive the gifts of the Spirit, we pray:

First Sunday of Lent, cycle C

That everyone who calls upon God's name, the followers of Christ and followers of Moses, be saved in the coming of the kingdom, we pray:

Second Sunday of Lent, cycle C

That the descendents of Abraham—Jews, Christians and Moslems—put on the faith of our father, we pray:

Third Sunday of Lent, cycle C

That we Christians acknowledge ourselves as the barren fig tree cluttering the ground and that we turn to God, our source of life, we pray:

Fourth Sunday of Lent, cycle C

For our Jewish brothers and sisters. that we reconcile with them in God's name, we pray:

Fifth Sunday of Lent, cycle C

That the people of Israel and the people of the church forgive each other from the heart, we pray:

Passion (Palm) Sunday, cycle C

That the well-trained tongue God gave us tell our Jewish brothers and sisters of our care for them, we pray:

Good Friday, cycle C
(See Good Friday, cycle A)

Easter Sunday, cycle C

That the Holy One of Israel, God of heaven and earth, bless all his faithful ones in churches, synagogues and temples on this day of days, we pray:

Second Sunday of Easter, cycle C

That Christians and Jews never again have reason to fear each other, we pray:

Third Sunday of Easter, cycle C

That Israel and the church together be brought to repentance and the forgiveness of sin, we pray:

Fourth Sunday of Easter, cycle C

That gentiles and Jews respond together to the word of the Lord with praise, we pray:

Fifth Sunday of Easter, cycle C

That the God of heaven and earth draw Israel and church to the new Jerusalem, where there is no more death or mourning, crying out or pain, we pray:

Sixth Sunday of Easter, cycle C

That the twelve tribes of Israel and all who follow the Lamb see the holy city Jerusalem and the splendor of God's name, we pray:

Seventh Sunday of Easter, cycle C

That Jewish people and Christian people prepare together for the day of the Lord, we pray:

Pentecost, cycle C

That with our brothers and sisters of Israel, we go forth in the Spirit to be instruments of peace, we pray:

James A. Wilde

Sample Reflections and Illustrations

Second Sunday of Advent, cycle A

Isaiah 11:1-10

Romans 15:4-9

Matthew 3:1-12

What do you think when you hear these verses from Isaiah? "On that day a shoot shall sprout . . . " Or: "Then the wolf shall be a guest of the lamb . . . " Or: "The earth shall be filled with knowledge of the Lord."

What do you think of?

Probably, like most Christians, you think in this Advent setting about Christmas coming, about Jesus. We have heard Isaiah's words as a fore-telling of Jesus Christ.

There are problems with this, problems that Paul was already strug-gling with. Paul tried in his letter to the Romans to work this out. Is it the question: What of the Jews? There's a little of that in today's second read-ing; "I affirm that Christ became the servant of the Jews because of God's faithfulness in fulfilling the promises to the patriarchs." Earlier in this same letter he wrote: "Is it possible that I, an Israelite, descended from Abraham through the tribe of Benjamin, could agree that God had rejected his people?" He then likens the gentile Christians (us) to a wild branch grafted to a tree that is Israel. "Remember," he says, "it is the root that supports you."

Remember. But we forgot. We took a Jewish prophet like Isaiah and decided he could only be talking about Jesus. And with all those clear prophecies, how could the Jews have missed the messiah? And Christians got into a habit of drawing old/new comparisons: the old way of the Jews being empty and sour, all in contrast to our shining selves.

Advent makes us face this. Our generation must do it with the holo-caust as witness. We can love Isaiah as a Jewish prophet talking to Jews, still. Vatican II taught that the writings of the prophets have their own value, *entirely apart from the Christian Scriptures*. And John Paul II has affirmed—along with the apostle Paul—that God's covenant with the Jews is a living reality.

What then of these Advent readings from Isaiah? Try reading it in light of what the Vatican Commission on Religious Relations with the Jews wrote last year: "Attentive to the same God who has spoken, hanging on the same word, we Jews and Christians have to witness to one same mem-ory and one common hope to Him who is master of history. We must also accept our responsibility to prepare the world for the coming of the Messiah by working together for social justice.''

To prepare the world for the coming of *whom*? And how? Now read Isaiah once more.

Gabe Huck, *At Home with the Word*

Third Sunday in Ordinary Time, cycle C

Nehemiah 8:2-4, 5-6, 8-10

1 Corinthians 12:12-30

Luke 1:1-4; 4:14-21

It is fascinating to watch the Hasidim study the scriptures. When these ultra-orthodox Jews study God's word, they do so privately, yet not alone. They usually stand before the table that contains the book, chanting the text in a low voice and bobbing constantly in a series of short bows. The chanting and the bowing are supposed to keep their attention focused on the text and to block out distractions.

But these activities have other consequences as well. The movement signals other Hasidim in the room that someone is studying the Bible. And if someone overhears a familiar or controversial text being chanted, he might wander over to discuss the text or to examine what the rabbis have said about the text. (The pronoun ''he'' is used deliberately; usually only men are allowed to study the scriptures publicly.)

What happens, then, is that this private study of scripture becomes a public event, one that is subject to the involvement of the community. The reasons for this are theological. First, the revelation was given to the whole people by God through Moses. ''Moses, with the elders of Israel, gave the people this order: 'Keep all these commandments which I enjoin on you today' '' (Deuteronomy 27:1). Second, this is the word of the Lord, which no one human being can interpret alone. We affirm our sense of the uniqueness of these words when we identify them as ''the word of the Lord'' at the end of each lesson.

This double sense of the community possession of the word and its unique nature is the source of our liturgical practice in the liturgy of the word. Here the word receives special treatment. It is proclaimed by someone who is specially prepared for the task. It is read from a special book and at a special place (bema, lectern, pulpit, ambo). Sometimes the word is chanted, or the book and readers are surrounded with candles and incense. Above all, it is proclaimed by a human voice in the midst of the assembly of believers. The people said to Moses, "You speak to us, and we will listen; but let not God speak to us, or we shall die" (Exodus 20:19).

The hearing of God's word in the assembly was behind the ritual at the Water Gate in today's first reading, as it was behind Jesus taking on the role of reader in the synagogue. In both instances, the holy word becomes accessible because it is also a human word. When proclaimed, it becomes the property of the whole people and not the private preserve of any one individual. It is a special word and deserves special treatment: it needs interpretation to make its meaning clear for "today."

Too often Christians forget their communal responsibility to the word. It is so accessible to us in contemporary translations and in inexpensive paperback editions that we are tempted to read it and reflect on it in private. Too often we use excerpts from it to prove our point and to batter other Christians into submission, forgetting that the whole of scripture must be kept in mind when interpreting each part. Too often we forget that the word needs a human voice to make it accessible to us, and yet that same word and that same voice must be treated with care and respect, for they bear the word of God.

The practice of the orthodox, the story of Ezra at the Water Gate, and the account of Jesus in the synagogue at Nazareth all serve to remind us of our identity as a community of the word. We are formed by that word; we are formed in that word in the midst of the assembly; we have no right to privatize that word or to destroy its integrity. We are, as Paul reminds us today, the body of Christ and individually members of it. It is Christ who speaks in us and through us; it is the spirit of Christ who brings the word to life in our hearts and in our community. We need not fear that word, for we are the body of Christ. We are the word of the Lord.

Dierdre Kriewald, *Homily Service*

Second Sunday of Lent, cycle C

Genesis 15:5-12, 17-18

Philippians 3:17—4:1

Luke 9:28-36

There are some strange stories in our book. Today we have two of them. First is Abraham. A wonderful first line: "God took Abraham outside." That's how the stories about Abraham are told. That's how it got repeated generation to generation: long ago, in our father Abraham's time, God was right there to say, "Come on, Abraham, let's go outside and look at the stars." Then five animals are slain, three of them split in half and Abraham sleeps until dark (even though earlier in the story he was counting the stars!). This is making a covenant: you split the dead animals in half and pass between the halves. If either of us breaks this bargain, may it happen to that one as it happened to this goat.

Why on earth do we bother to tell such a story? It was an old tale already when Moses lived. That is perhaps part of what is to be treasured about all the Abraham stories: they were told in the slave quarters in Egypt, told hundreds of years later in the promised land, told in Babylon when Abraham's descendants were taken there captive, told after the return and during the years when Greeks and Romans lorded it over Israel. Soon thereafter they were being told not by one people but by two and then by three as Christians and Moslems took to themselves the Abraham stories.

So we have this ancestor honored on both sides of many battles, by Christian inquisitors and Jewish martyrs, by devout Arab Moslems and devout Jews. Now they have been told again in death camps of Nazi Germany, repeated in a reborn Israel, pondered by Christians in tiny communities in Latin America and Africa.

All have puzzled over Abraham and called him father, this wandering immigrant whom God liked to take outside to count stars. One thing we do in Lent is attend to our roots, find what we have in our genes. How is this a vital part of what Paul advises us to do in the second reading?

Gabe Huck, *At Home with the Word*

Fourth Sunday of Lent, cycle A

1 Samuel 16:1, 6-7, 10-13

Ephesians 5:8-14

John 9:1-41

Something in John's way of writing is all the more dangerous because we get so accustomed to it that we don't even notice. Halfway through the story we find this line: "The Jews refused to believe that he had really been born blind." And a little later: "His parents . . . were afraid of the Jews."

Who refused to believe? Of *whom* were the parents afraid?

The text says simply "the Jews."

But what can the author mean? Every single person in this story is a Jew: the Pharisees, the parents, the disciples, the man himself, and, of course, Jesus. So what sort of sense does it make to say that "the Jews" refused to believe?

John uses this sweeping designation to describe not *all* the Jews in the immediate story he is telling, but just some or a few of the characters. This is especially true in the narrative of the passion. Scholars have offered various explanations of this use of a word that implicates the whole people when only a few are intended. John wrote at a time when there had been much antagonism between the vast majority of Jews who rejected the claims made by the followers of Jesus, and those few Jews and many gentiles who called Jesus their savior.

Does this antagonism then come out in John's retelling of the stories? That would be one explanation for the way he so often seems to separate Jesus from other Jews, and to write as if incidents like the curing of this man's blindness set off Jews against non-Jews (when in fact all the characters are Jews). All of this must be seen against another side of John. It is certainly a paradox that it is this evangelist who puts on Jesus' lips these words: "After all, salvation is from the Jews."

It is all too clear which side of John's ambiguous feelings has been handed on to us. Only in recent decades have there been beginnings at teaching Christians about a Jewish Jesus, a Jesus who cannot be understood in the categories of the Greeks or Romans, but only in the categories of the Jewish Bible from which he learned to live and to pray and to teach.

Even in telling of a man born blind, the storyteller and his community didn't see all that clearly. It is a wonderful story, a fitting story for this midpoint of Lent. In Lent we are meant to face all those ways in which "the night comes on when on one can work." We are meant to face—all of us (let's include John the evangelist)—that we mostly say, "We see!" when we have not yet been touched by the mud and word of Jesus. We will treasure the story, but try to remember that even a story tells a story.

Gabe Huck, *At Home with the Word*

Palm Sunday, cycle A

Isaiah 50:4-7

Philippians 2:6-11

Matthew 26:14—27:66

It is Matthew's passion account we read this Sunday for this is the year of reading Matthew beginning to end. And what is unique in this account? What are some of the things Matthew narrates that others omit? Only Matthew has the aside about Pilate's wife and her dream. Only Matthew has Pilate wash his hands. In these little incidents, as in much of the dialogue in the story, Matthew seems to take pains to get the Romans off the hook.

There is, on Matthew's part, a lot of hindsight here. The little Christian churches for whom Matthew wrote were trying to get along in the Roman Empire. They weren't anxious to antagonize Romans. In fact, they were out to convert Romans to the gospel. They had turned their back on the Jewish people. The truth seems to be that with the Romans occupying and ruling the land, it is they who would have had all responsibility in the arrest and execution of Jesus, probably with the assistance of a few Jewish collaborators.

So it is best perhaps not to read too much into Matthew's efforts at good public relations with the Romans. Ponder instead the passion of Jesus through the eyes of Paul as we do in the second reading. Paul felt no need to know or tell any details, no need to cast blame. Rather he tried to say what he believed. And so should we. How then does Paul see it? And we?

Gabe Huck, *At Home with the Word*

Palm Sunday, cycle B

Isaiah 50:4-7

Philippians 2:6-11

Mark 14:1—15:47

This Sunday is a strong and final preparation. Life and death are players here, but that's easy to say when we think we know how the story comes out. We don't know. We don't *know*. How we *believe* and how we *behave* are more to the point.

Read what Isaiah said. Why bother to repeat these words every year? Is it because of the "I gave my back" verse? Only in a way. Lots of Jewish backs were beaten and lots of Jewish faces spit upon in Isaiah's time and in Jesus' time. And in our time, far worse. Jesus was treated like so many, many others when he spoke and acted like one of God's free people. The Romans, the oppressors of the moment, would have none of it.

We read it over again because we need to face that Jewish Jesus who learned freedom and suffering and the great mystery of God's covenant.

How have we followed him? This week, at the liturgies of Holy Thursday and Good Friday and especially at the Easter Vigil we will read the book that he read. We will read from Genesis and Exodus, Isaiah and Ezekiel. Are we ready to listen to the word found there?

Gabe Huck, *At Home with the Word*

Good Friday

Isaiah 52:13—53:12

Hebrews 4:14-16; 5:7-9

John 18:1—19:42

There is an unspoken bond between a rapidly aging generation of certain Jews and certain gentiles who survived the Second World War. It is a bond of hopelessness, disbelief and murdered faith. They stay shy from synagogues or churches. Prayer will not come to their lips. They suffer similar dreams. Loud noises, knocks on the door, or policemen bring them irrational fears.

Many were strapped to chairs while their fingernails were torn out or their teeth smashed. Many kept vigil while relatives or neighbors died in agony from beatings. Many survived eating their own pets. Many lived hidden in the rubble of demolished towns.

On Good Friday we tell of three people tortured and murdered. Three people. Yet this generation of survivors can tell of hundreds, not from a book, but from the memory of faces and the sound of voices in the nightmare of their destruction.

If we dare stand up to preach, if we dare to put prayers on other people's lips, we cannot speak for this generation without being one with them, seeing what they should never have seen, knowing what no human being should ever know.

Peter Mazar

The passion narrative according to John is so vast a tapestry that only a few aspects can be featured here. It presents a Jesus who is fully aware of his own fate (18:4), before whom his would-be captors fall to the ground in dismay (v. 6), and who magisterially instructs Pilate more than the prefect interrogates him (18:33-38; 19:9-11).

After Jesus' capture in a place familiar to Judas (18:2), Jesus is led "first" to Annas who appears only here and without previous introduction (v. 13). He is correctly identified as the father-in-law of Caiaphas, whom we know from Josephus to have been the high priest at the time. It was not an annual office, hence the phrase describing the son-in-law's tenure is probably to be translated "in that fateful year." John 11:46-57 seems to be a sentence of death passed on Jesus by Caiaphas or at least the sealing of his doom, which is plotted carefully in this gospel from 5:18 onward. This may account for the relative brevity of the hearing before Annas ("the high priest" — 18:19-24) and the suppression of any appearance before Caiaphas, the actual office-holder (vv. 24, 28).

Peter's cowardly denial (vv. 15-18) contrasts with Jesus' brave stand before his captors (vv. 5-8) and before Annas (vv. 19-23), as in the synoptics. If the "other disciple" of verse 15 were "the disciple whom Jesus loved" it would serve to authenticate the narrative. Attractive as the hypothesis is, it cannot be proved. As to Jesus' response to the high priest regarding his "teaching" (the teaching of the Johannine community, very probably), one gathers from it that the essential issues between Jesus and "the Jews" have already been debated and decided—chiefly in chapters 7 through 10—leaving Jesus' answer in vv. 20-21 as John's summary of that situation.

The Roman trial before Pilate is markedly different from the Jewish hearing. It is a superb example of the evangelist's literary and theological genius and is not to be confused with the *genre* of history—apart from the fact that Pilate did sentence Jesus to death ("delivered him over to be crucified," 19:16). The main interest is in the scenes where Jesus and Pilate are alone on the stage: 18:33-38*b* and 19:8-12*a*. There we find theological discussions on the nature of Jesus' kingship, on truth (the Johannine *alētheia*, not philosophical truth) and authority from above—again, not that granted by the Roman state but by God who is the chief author of the drama.

Any pulpit treatment of this powerful narrative that sees in it a history of Jesus' last hours misconceives it. An exploration of its themes which sees them consistent with the entire gospel that precedes them is on the right track. And a reading of the passion that recognizes it as both cosmic and existential for Christian communities like John's and the homilist's is dealing with it correctly. The "world"—all that is set against God's truth in Jesus—is the sole enemy in the play, not Judas or Pilate or Simon Peter or the crowd. Cosmic sin is pitted against total innocence.

"And the Slain hath the gain, and the Victor hath the rout."

Cynthia Bourgeault, *Homily Service*

The immediate response when one feels outrage is to look for someone to blame. For most of our Christian era, the blame for the crucifixion fell on the Jews, and Good Friday became the quintessence of the church's anti-Semitic stance.

Within our still anguished memories, two thousand years of anti-Semitism reached their grotesque culmination in the holocaust. Today, as the human race again faces genocide in the form of nuclear weaponry, we must—at last—hear the message of this day. The crucifixion is not about placing blame; it celebrates God's redemptive power in the world, and is inseparable from Easter. It is not about abandonment, but about love bridging the void.

Cynthia Bourgeault, *Homily Service*

Third Sunday of Easter, cycle A

Acts 2:14, 22-28

1 Peter 1:17-21

Luke 24:13-35

There is a restless problem sitting in the middle of our Eastertime. The readings this Sunday point right to it. It is the separation of two peoples. Consider these items:

- "You even used pagans to crucify and kill him." (First reading)
- "How our chief priests and leaders delivered him up to be condemned to death." (Gospel)

In a very long and very powerful documentary movie called "Shoah," the movie's director interviews some older residents of a Polish town. This town was the location of a concentration camp during World War II. The Jews of this town and of many towns—400,000 Jews in all—were brought here and were systematically executed. The people interviewed were young then, but they remember when they played and worked with Jews in the days before the war. And they remember how the Jews were penned up in the village church and starved there until the gas vans took them to their graves in the forest. The village people saw it all. There have been no Jews in the village—where Jews had lived for hundreds of years—since then. They speak about those days and about the screaming they would hear. Life has gone on.

Why did it happen? One woman recalls the scriptures they have heard all their lives (and that we heard three weeks ago today): "His blood be on us and on our children." Others nod.

The wrong thing to do would be to sneer at these people, at their use of the scriptures, at their willingness to worship weekly in a church which was in their own lifetimes the brutal prison for adults and children condemned to die simply for being Jews. Perhaps these people could have done something to stop it, but they were also without real power, ruled and controlled by occupying forces.

What should frighten us in this scene from "Shoah" is that Christians are still voicing Jewish guilt for the death of Christ. This is what Christians were taught. Was such teaching the cause or even the condition that allowed the Nazis to set up whole systems—the railroads, the camps, the theft and distribution of the Jews' property—to murder six million Jews from all parts of Europe, from the towns that had been their homes for hundreds of years? Most Christians just watched.

Perhaps we should no longer read aloud those parts of the scriptures which speak as if the Jewish people were responsible for Jesus' death. The church has officially repudiated this view. Passages like this one from Acts were written long after the fact, long after Jews and Christians had parted ways and began to speak hatefully of one another.

Or if we do read them, we might read them on our knees. We are not the ones who did it. No, but we have yet to grapple with what has happened. We call these scriptures our own. They may mean something different for us than for any previous generation.

Gabe Huck, *At Home with the Word*

Third Sunday of Easter, cycle B

Acts 3:13-15, 17-19

1 John 2:1-5a

Luke 24:35-48

By the time most of the letters and stories and gospels of the Christian Scriptures were written down, a very important and tragic development had taken place among the followers of Jesus. Can you find signs of it in today's readings?

We know that those Jews who followed the Jew Jesus had various expectations. We know that they, like many other groups at the time, believed the hour had come for some turn in Israel's history, that the Roman oppression and the collaboration and softness of some of their own leaders must end. In the years after Jesus' execution, these disciples of Jesus had to find a place and a meaning for themselves.

They preached Jesus as savior. They said that these years were but a short space before he returned to set things right. They preached this to Jews, but their listeners had heard many such claims. In some places, great hostilities developed. And more and more, the "Christian" Jews took their message to other peoples.

Can you see in the first reading and gospel what eventually happened? Jesus' execution had been one more Roman act to control a rebellious people. It made no great impression on the Romans and, for the Jews, it was simply another brutal deed of the occupying empire. But now, in these readings, it is being used much later by followers of Jesus not against the Romans and the few collaborators, but against the whole Jewish people! The sermon Peter gives is the way things seemed to later generations: "You put to death the leader of life." He attributed it to ignorance, but the charge of "godkiller" would ring for 19 centuries—till now!—on the lips of Christians. And Jewish men and women, children and infants would be insulted, oppressed, abused and murdered as a result. Hitler told some bishops he was only putting into practice what the church had taught all along. Was he right?

Ironically, the scriptures of Eastertime more than of any other season raise the tragedy of Christian failures. How are we heirs in our own thoughts and words to this sad history? What can we hope for?

Gabe Huck, *At Home with the Word*

In Acts 3 Jesus, "the honored servant of God," leads "the way to life." The art of rhetoric is evident here. The contrast between the murderer set free and the murdered author of life is too dramatic to be soon forgotten, but it is not the end of the story. The point for Peter is not who killed Jesus but who can recognize the source of true power and godliness in this season of wonder and amazement.

Rachel Reeder, *Homily Service*

Fourth Sunday of Easter, cycle C

Acts 13:14, 43-52

Revelation 7:9, 14-17

John 10:27-30

"My sheep hear my voice. I know them and they follow me. I give them eternal life." Audacious words from Jesus, but there is more to come. If the crowd is wondering how Jesus can dare promise eternal life, he answers plainly: "The Father and I are one." Not surprisingly, John's next sentence reports that "the Jews fetched stones to stone him." This messiah is making claims that transcend, indeed undermine, the narrow vision of the audience that the fourth evangelist calls "the Jews." In bringing John's text to our own world, there are two things to be said. One is a word of warning, the other is a word of hope.

When John's gospel speaks of "the Jews," it opens the door to a cancer that has plagued the church since the beginning, the disease of anti-Semitism. The problem is compounded when we hear from Paul, as in Acts 13, about how the sons and daughters of Abraham rejected Paul's message. We must remember that such texts mean, even if they fail to say it with precision, "some of the Jews." All of the twelve, along with Mary the mother of Jesus and the overwhelming majority of the first believers, were Jews. Anti-Semitic Christians are not only in clear opposition to Jesus' teaching about loving one's neighbor, they blatantly contradict the historical roots of our faith. Without Judaism, the gospel is unintelligible. Without Jews like John and Paul, we would not know the good news. In short, there is really only one just and correct response of Christianity to Judaism—gratitude.

The narrowness of anti-Semitism finds its antidote in the message of hope in today's readings—the good news about the breadth of God's love. Revelation speaks about "a huge crowd which no one could count from every nation and race, people and tongue." The community of the saved is open to everyone. This teaching is fundamental, woven into the very fabric of the gospel. God is a lover and God's love knows no bounds. Love's arms embrace the whole human family. Its vision transcends the narrowness of our prejudices and divisions. God's love is indiscriminate, and we who are made in God's image are called to love in the same way.

Joseph Serano, *Homily Service*

Sixth Sunday of Easter, cycle C

Acts 15:1-2, 22-29
Revelation 21:10-14, 22-23
John 14:23-29

A story is always told from hindsight. The teller knows the outcome; the outcome shapes the telling. So today we have a story from the Acts of the Apostles. The stage is set with characters and controversy. Paul and Barnabas are on one side. They are preaching Jesus to the gentiles and saying that these non-Jews can belong to God's kingdom without fulfilling all the Jewish law. On the other side are some anonymous evangelists, missionaries, who dispute this. They would have all those who believe in Jesus belong fully to the Jewish community.

Hindsight sets the stage so clearly and sharply. The storyteller also knows about suspense: the two factions send delegates to Jerusalem to see the apostles and to argue the case. In Jerusalem the question is debated and a decision is reached: non-Jews who are baptized into the Christian communities need not take on all of the facets and practices of Jewish life.

So do great struggles, much trouble, painful and anguished years of argument come to be summed up in a little story. From here, we hardly understand what all the arguing was about. It seems much ado about something very obvious. But consider what it was like at the time. Who could understand Jesus of Nazareth apart from what he was? And what he was was a Jew, faithful to the law and prophets in life and in death, a Jew whose zeal for the kingdom of God—the God of his Jewish parents and ancestors—brought him to the fatal attention of the civil authorities, the Romans who occupied the nation. How could one preach Jesus and not the Jewish way of life, the law he studied and loved, the sabbath that God had fashioned for this people?

But in those years there was also this other question: why did so few Jews join the little communities in which Jesus was acclaimed as the child of God, the savior? And when Jesus was preached to non-Jews, why did so many put their faith in him? The pondering and arguing about this went on and on. If we are not to find God as Jesus found God—that is, by walking in the way of Jesus, then what way can we walk, those of us born outside the Jewish community? What things should we reject from our old ways? All of this took decades to work out. The story today just sums it up: "It is the decision of the Holy Spirit, and ours too, not to lay on you any burden beyond that which is strictly necessary, namely, to abstain from meat sacrificed to idols, from blood, from the meat of strangled animals, and from illicit sexual union." They were working things out. Slowly.

But hindsight also tells us that it didn't work out. Many Jewish communities each year keep a day of remembrance called Yom Hashoah: the Day of Holocaust. It comes twelve days after Passover, and it is an addition made to the Jewish calendar in our generation to remember the six million, the entire Jewish civilization in the midst of Christian Europe, who were put to death during our lives or the lives of our parents.

What had happened between these two peoples, the people to whom Jesus belonged and the people who called Jesus Lord? In the first generations they could not understand each other. Paul wrote to the church at Rome that they, the gentiles, are but wild branches grafted on the tree. Remember, he told them, it is not you that support the root, but the root that supports you: the Jews are God's people and God has not rejected them. But that was a hard teaching, forgotten by most Christians until remorse for our own silence during the holocaust drove us to see that we had for centuries taught contempt. Christian anti-Semitic teachings permitted some to stand by silently and others to join in the genocide.

This tradition is not over so long as we speak in stereotypes of Jews, whether in jest, in meanness, or just in the routine of things. The teaching of contempt goes on when we presume that Jews do not remain the people of God's covenant, when we speak as if that covenant had been somehow canceled. It was hard in those first generations to know what to do, and it is hard now. We can at least do this: be silent for a while with our brothers and sisters, and ponder what has happened in our time. The very joy of the Easter season must be altered by such sorrow.

Gabe Huck, *Homily Service*

Twenty-second Sunday in Ordinary Time, cycle B

Deuteronomy 4:1-2, 6-8

James 1:17-18, 21b-22, 27

Mark 7:1-8, 14-15, 21-23

The reading from the Gospel of Mark is strong but easily misunderstood. The selection from Deuteronomy must be part of our effort to comprehend Mark. If you think that the Law (the commandments within the whole Torah) was a burden or a punishment, something oppressive, then read these lines of Deuteronomy with care. Which lines do you find especially moving? What sort of relation is there between Israel and God? This "Law" was a way of life, a way for Israel to walk. To keep the Law was to live by the covenant, to be bound to the Lord.

Jesus knew the Law as such a total way of life and lived by it. His teaching, like that of many other zealous Jews of his day, struggled with what fidelity to Israel's God meant. How should we live now? How are we to keep the covenant? How are those words of Deuteronomy still true?

The Pharisees come off poorly in Mark and even worse in the other gospels, but in fact we know that their approach was not much different from that of Jesus. Later, when the gospels were written, the differences were greatly exaggerated. We continue a great injustice when we make "Pharisee" another word for hypocrite.

The everlasting problem is our behavior. Jesus and the Pharisees were both struggling with that. By coincidence today, the second reading is also on this track. How do the words of James and Jesus cut into our lives?

Gabe Huck, *At Home with the Word*

Our gospel today gives us yet another of the many stories of Jesus *versus* the Pharisees, and as usual, the Pharisees fall flat on their faces. Most of us have a rather stereotyped picture of the Pharisees, one heavily reinforced by movie and TV specials. We imagine them as haughty, corpulent, smug—the obvious fall guy. From our own vantage point of two thousand years' hindsight, it is hard to envision how they could have been so blind as to have missed the son of God walking right in their midst. We chuckle with approval as Jesus the liberator sets his people free from dietary fetishes. "It's not what goes into a person that defiles the person, but what comes out of the person."

A more careful look at history, however, gives us a rather different picture of the Pharisees—with some thought-provoking implications for our own time. The Pharisees were the religious enlightenment of their times. They were attempting to breathe new life into a faith that for many had become no more than a jumble of half-forgotten rules and habits. As educators, they were trying to recapture the living spirit of their religion, to feel tradition as a living vessel into which God poured life. The old forms were not dead, claimed the Pharisees, but vibrant channels of the presence of God. That is why Jesus' seemingly casual disregard for these forms evoked from them such fierce hostility and anguish.

In this light it is possible to view the consternation which Jesus causes them a bit more sympathetically. Suppose you were at a conference on the eucharist, exploring and celebrating the profound meaning of this ancient rite. And just as you were really getting caught up in the spirit of it, some unknown upstart leaped to the podium and announced, "It is not what goes into a person that unites one to God; it's what comes out of a person." How would you feel? Cheated? Does that make you a Pharisee?

The point of this comparison is that in our gospel today we are not just dealing with "good guys" and "bad guys" but with a fundamental tension of religious life. Borrowing from the gospel for the Feast of the Transfiguration, we might call it the "three tabernacles syndrome." No sooner have we been swept with the religious fire than we want to erect some monument to the experience—be it a tabernacle, a liturgy, or a church. And that tabernacle does, in fact, become a living channel of religious experience; a way to celebrate and share the faith. But at the same time, that tabernacle pointing to the thing itself is not the thing itself, and if we forget this essential distinction, we slip noiselessly from faith into idolatry. The living symbols that give form and coherence to our search for God become, ultimately, the greatest roadblocks to that search.

Is there a way out of this trap? One way is the route of iconoclasm. Iconoclasts build no forms, make no liturgies, leave no traces. They ponder only the dark and ineffable God, whose presence shatters every human tabernacle.

An alternate way is the route of incarnation. In a world in which not even God escapes crucifixion, this is a route of great courage and pain. We live only to have our traditions broken and our hearts broken. Again and again the overarching presence of the spirit shatters our tabernacles, makes mockery of our most deeply held pieties, teases and twists us always onward in a seemingly breathless race, causing us to create new forms and almost as quickly to abandon these creations. This is almost iconoclasm, except for one thing: the race itself is the living presence of God. It is the throbbing pulse of a heart which longs to give itself utterly to us, to make us ever more and ever deeper a part of the holy love which is beyond form but never without it.

Harry Kiely, *Homily Service*

Sample Bulletin Items

Racism and anti-Semitism can be one of our hardest sins to uproot. One small, positive step is to make sure that images of minorities are in our home. For example, some of the pictures, works of art or religious images in our home might depict these minorities or their cultures. We might consider subscribing to a publication like *Ebony, Ebony, Jr., Nuestro* or a Jewish-oriented periodical like *Commentary, Jewish Currents, Judaica Book News, Moment, Sentinel* or *Modern Hebrew Literature.*

> Anne Wolf, *At Home with the Word*

There is only one really important ecumenical question: our relationship with Judaism.

> Karl Barth (in his 1966 visit to the Vatican Secretariat
> for Promoting Christian Unity)

A unique goal underlies the Jewish-Christian encounter. The church realizes that just as her roots are to be found in the revelation of God to Israel on Sinai, so even today the church draws sustenance from the root of that well-cultivated olive tree onto which have been grafted the wild shoots, the gentiles.

> *Nostra Aetate,* #4, Vatican Council II

Do you know who said that the Old Testament really is not the word of God as the New Testament is? Who said that the Old Testament is only about law and justice while the New is about love and mercy? Who taught that the New Testament abrogated or superseded the Old Testament? Who? The answer is: Marcion, a second century religious leader from Asia Minor (today's Turkey), whose views were condemned as heretical by the church and whom some faithful Christians called "first born of Satan."

> James A. Wilde

He who does not increase his knowledge diminishes it. He who does not study deserves to die.

> Rabbi Hillel, *Palestinian Talmud*

The Jews have been God's chosen people for centuries, yet they continue to be persecuted in the world. Christians have often rationalized their own anti-Semitism by pointing to Jesus' crucifixion. Reflect on your own attitudes towards Jews. Do you believe many of the stereotypes? What one action can you take to overcome your own anti-Semitism?

Anne Wolf, At Home with the Word

The New Testament does not present history in our sense of the term. It reveals the *meaning* of history. As revelation, it is not intended to give us merely a listing of facts and events. Rather it aims to teach us the salvific will of God that underlines all events. It reveals to us our *own* sins and our *own* salvation. To the question "Who killed Jesus?" the Christian replies "I did."

Eugene Fisher, Faith Without Prejudice

Our common Judeo-Christian heritage impels us toward this, our common heritage of service to humanity and its immense spiritual and material needs. Through different but finally convergent ways we will be able to reach, with the help of the Lord who has never ceased loving his people (cf. Romans 11:1), this true brotherhood in reconciliation and respect, and to contribute to a full implementation of God's plan in history.

Pope John Paul II, 6 March 1982

When Abbot Bernard of Clairvaux was commissioned by Pope Eugenius III in 1145 to preach the second crusade, he gained many recruits by announcing that killing an infidel would merit a place in heaven. Rudolph, a Cistercian monk who left Clairvaux to enlist recruits in Germany for the rescue of the Holy Land, told the German masses it was their duty to kill first the enemies of Christ in their own country. He told his congregations that these infidels—violent men and well armed—were a long way off and that it was much safer and equally meritorious to kill unarmed Jews at home.

Rabbi Marc Tanenbaum

The dead of Auschwitz should have changed everything, and nothing should have been able to continue as before, neither among our people nor within our churches, especially within our churches! They at least should have perceived the spiritual catastrophe that Auschwitz signified which has left neither our people nor our community unscathed. Instead, what point have we in fact reached, we Christians and middle-class citizens of this country? Not only the point where all has once more become as it was in the beginning, with Auschwitz considered as merely an incident, however deplorable, in the day's work! Already today there are growing signs of a

65

new climate of thought in which the causes for the terror of Auschwitz are being sought, not only among the assassins and persecutors, but also among their victims and the persecuted.

Johannes B. Metz, Concilium

Christian theology after Auschwitz must be guided by the understanding that Christians can only comprehend their own identity in the presence of the Jewish people. Christian theology can preserve its identity only when faced with the history of the faith of the Jews and in relationship to it. With this object in view, Christian theology must re-evaluate the Jewish dimension present in Christian faith and overcome the barrier which imprisons the Jewish heritage present in Christianity. It is called upon to rediscover in a special way the biblical messianic dimension.

Johannes B. Metz, Concilium

After the Holocaust, how can we imagine or conceive of a God who did not save under those circumstances? In what sort of language might we even frame these questions and to whom might we address them? Have not the very coherence of language and the continuity of traditions been broken, shattered by this event?

Susan Shapiro, Concilium

PART FOUR

A Vatican Tradition Unfolds

James A. Wilde

Calendar of Offical and Semi-official Catholic Statements on Jewish-Christian Relations: 1965-1985

1965   *Declaration on the Relation of the Church to Non-Christian Religions* (Nostra Aetate)
Vatican Council II

1973   *Pastoral Orientations on the Attitude of Christians to Judaism*
National Conference of French Bishops

1975   *Guidelines and Suggestions for Implementing the Conciliar Declaration* Nostra Aetate, *#4*
Vatican Commission for Religious Relations with the Jews

Statement on Catholic-Jewish Relations,
National Conference of United States Bishops

"Address to the American Jewish Committee"
Archbishop Joseph Bernardin

"Guidelines"
Archdiocese of Galveston-Houston

"On Israel and the U.N."
Archbishop Joseph Bernardin

"On the U.N. Vote on Zionism"
Archbishop Joseph Bernardin

1977   "The Mission and Witness of the Church"
Professor Tommaso Federici, Member
Vatican Commission for Religious Relations with the Jews

"Catechetics and Judaism"
John Cardinal Willebrands, President
Vatican Secretariat for Christian Unity

"Guidelines"
Archdiocese of Los Angeles

1979   Homily at Auschwitz
Pope John Paul II

"Statement on the Seder Celebration"
Archdiocese of Louisville

"Guidelines"
Diocese of Brooklyn

"Guidelines"
Diocese of Cleveland

"Guidelines"
Archdiocese of Detroit

Basic Theological Issues of Jewish-Christian Dialogue
Central Committee of Roman Catholics in Germany

1980   Address to the Jewish Community, Mainz, West Germany
Pope John Paul II

The Church and the Jews
National Conference of German Bishops

"Guidelines"
Diocese of Trenton

1981   "A Renewed Vision of Catholic-Jewish Relations"
Address to the Executive Committee of the
Synagogue Council of America
Archbishop John R. Roach

1982   Address to Delegates of Episcopal Conferences on Relations
with Judaism
Pope John Paul II

1983   "Reconciliation with the Jewish People"
Intervention at the Synod of Bishops on Reconciliation, Rome
Roger Cardinal Etchegaray, Marseilles

Orientations for Catholic-Jewish Dialogue
National Conference of Brazilian Bishops

"Ecumenical Guidelines"
Diocese of Rome

"Guidelines for Jewish-Catholic Marriages"
Archdiocese of Newark

1984   "The Catholic Style: A Reflection on the Documents"
Msgr. Jorge Mejia, Executive Secretary
Vatican Commission for Religious Relations with the Jews

"The State of Jewish-Christian Relations"
Address to the Eighth National Workshop on Jewish-Christian
Relations
Bishop James Malone

Redemptionis Anno
Pope John Paul II

Address to International Council of Christians and Jews
Pope John Paul II

1985   *Notes on the Correct Way to Present the Jews and Judaism in Preaching and Catechesis in the Roman Catholic Church*
Vatican Commission for Religious Relations with the Jews

Guidelines for Catholic-Jewish Relations: 1985 Revision
National Conference of United States Bishops

1986   "The Church and the Jewish Community"
Address to Jewish leaders in Sydney, Australia
Pope John Paul II

A comparison of the above-cited statements with similar statements by various member countries of the World Council of Churches and other Protestant groups of the United States and Europe is highly illuminating. The reader is referred to the handy compilation in two volumes by Helga Croner, entitled *Stepping Stones to Further Jewish-Christian Relations* and *More Stepping Stones to Jewish-Christian Relations,* published by Paulist Press.

An Unfolding Tradition

Over the past generation, the issue of Jewish-Catholic relations has been addressed in several different ways by the Vatican. Beginning with *Nostra Aetate* (*Declaration on the Relation of the Church to Non-Christian Religions*) of Vatican Council II in 1965, a fuller and clearer picture of the desired direction of those relations began to emerge.

The 1975 Vatican *Guidelines and Suggestions for Implementing the Conciliar Declaration Nostra Aetate, #4*, and the 1985 *Notes on the Correct Way to Present the Jews and Judaism in Preaching and Catechesis in the Roman Catholic Church* built on Vatican II and developed the tradition further. Meanwhile, Pope John Paul II shed light on the developing tradition at several points. In what follows, as a summary of what has preceded, these three declarations and some of Pope John Paul's insights will be compared in order to set into clear relief the dimensions of this tradition. A schematization of some of the following material is presented by Eugene J. Fisher in "The Development of a Tradition" (*SIDIC* 19:2, 1986, pages 20-23).

Nostra Aetate, *#4, Vatican Council II, 1965*

All preachers and teachers are invited to read the eight relevant paragraphs of *Nostra Aetate*, #4, which are presented here:

4. Sounding the depths of the mystery which is the church, this sacred Council remembers the spiritual ties which link the people of the New Covenant to the stock of Abraham.

The church of Christ acknowledges that in God's plan of salvation the beginning of her faith and election is to be found in the patriarchs, Moses and the prophets. She professes that all Christ's faithful, who as men of faith are sons of Abraham (cf. Galatians 3:7), are included in the same patriarch's call and that the salvation of the church is mystically prefigured in the exodus of God's chosen people from the land of bondage. On this account the church cannot forget that she received the revelation of the Old Testament by way of that people with whom God in his inexpressible mercy established the ancient covenant. Nor can she forget that she draws nourishment from the good olive tree onto which the wild olive branches of the Gentiles have been grafted (cf. Romans 11:17-24). The church believes that Christ who is our peace has through his cross reconciled Jews and Gentiles and made them one in himself (cf. Ephesians 2:14-16).

Likewise, the church keeps ever before her mind the words of the apostle Paul about his kinsmen: "they are Israelites, and to them belong the sonship, the glory, the covenants, the giving of the law, the worship, and the promises; to them belong the patriarchs, and of their race according to the flesh, is the Christ" (Romans 9:4-5), the son of the virgin Mary. She is mindful, moreover, that the apostles, the pillars on which the church stands, are of Jewish descent, as are many of those early disciples who proclaimed the gospel of Christ to the world.

As holy Scripture testifies, Jerusalem did not recognize God's moment when it came (cf. Luke 19:42). Jews for the most part did not accept the Gospel; on the contrary, many opposed the spreading of it (Romans 11:28). Even so, the apostle Paul maintains that the Jews remain very dear to God, for the sake of the patriarchs, since God does not take back the gifts he bestowed or the choice he made. Together with the prophets and that same apostle, the church awaits the day, known to God alone, when all peoples will call on God with one voice and "serve him shoulder to shoulder" (Zephaniah 3:9; cf. Isaiah 66:23; Psalms 65:4; Romans 11:11-32).

Since Christians and Jews have such a common spiritual heritage, this sacred Council wishes to encourage and further mutual understanding and appreciation. This can be obtained, especially, by way of biblical and theological inquiry and through friendly discussions.

Even though the Jewish authorities and those who followed their lead pressed for the death of Christ (cf John 19:6), neither all Jews indiscriminately at that time, nor Jews today, can be charged with the crimes committed during his passion. It is true that the church is the new people of God, yet the Jews should not be spoken of as rejected or accursed as if this followed from holy Scripture. Consequently, all must take care, lest in catechizing or in preaching the Word of God, they teach anything which is not in accord with the truth of the gospel message or the spirit of Christ.

Indeed, the church reproves every form of persecution against whomsoever it may be directed. Remembering, then, her common heritage with the Jews and moved not by any political consideration, but solely by the religious motivation of Christian charity, she deplores all hatreds, persecutions, displays of antisemitism leveled at any time or from any source against the Jews.

The church always held and continues to hold that Christ out of infinite love freely underwent suffering and death because of the sins of all men, so that all might attain salvation. It is the duty of the church, therefore, in her preaching to proclaim the cross of Christ as the sign of God's universal love and the source of all grace.

In these paragraphs, a twenty-century history reversed itself: Vatican II decried all forms of persecution and manifestation of anti-Semitism leveled at any time or from any source against the Jews. It further asserted that the crucifixion of Jesus cannot be blamed on all Jews then living without distinction nor upon the Jews of today. At last!

Nostra Aetate, #4 does the following:

- It acknowledges that the church received the revelation of God in the Hebrew Scriptures from Israel.
- It points to the fact that the church draws nourishment from that good olive tree onto which she has been grafted (cf. Romans 11:17-24).
- It recognizes with the apostle Paul about his kinsmen: "they are Israelites, and to them belong the sonship, the glory, the covenants, the giving of the law, the worship, and the promises; to them belong the patriarchs, and of their race according to the flesh, is the Christ" (Romans 9:4-5).
- It acknowledges that the apostles, the early pillars of the church, are of Jewish descent.
- It agrees with Paul that Jews remain very dear to God (Romans 11:11-32).
- It states that the church and Judaism together await the Day of the Lord.
- It advocates improved relations with Jewish people by way of biblical and theological inquiry and friendly discussion.
- It brings to the attention of all Catholics—and the whole world—an official end of an era and beginning of a new direction.

What *Nostra Aetate* does *not* do, however, includes the following:

- It makes no mention of the post-biblical religious tradition of Judaism.
- It makes no mention of the false stereotyping of the Pharisees or the misunderstandings that can arise from reading the Christian Scriptures or from the liturgy.
- It makes no reference to the State of Israel.
- It does not deal as such with the promise/fulfillment theme of the Christian Scriptures.
- It does not deal with typology.
- There is no reference to the joint witness to the world of the Jewish/Christian tradition.
- There is no explicit acknowledgment of the validity of the ongoing Jewish witness to the church or the world after Jesus' time.

Vatican Guidelines, 1975

Ten years after *Nostra Aetate*, the Vatican issued *Guidelines and Suggestions for Implementing the Conciliar Declaration* Nostra Aetate, #4, as an elaboration and clarification of some of the issues in the council's declaration. Published by the special Vatican Commission for Religious Relations with the Jews, established by Pope Paul VI in 1974, the *Guidelines* take another step forward in the developing tradition. They "fill in" some of the points left "creatively vague" by Vatican II.

First, the Vatican *Guidelines* place *Nostra Aetate* historically in the context of the holocaust:

> The step taken by the council finds its historical setting in circumstances deeply affected by the memory of the persecution and massacre of Jews which took place in Europe just before and during the Second World War.

The language of reconciliation, with such admissions as "ignorance" and "confrontation," sets a tone for dialogue.

Second, the urgency for improved relations is located at a deep level, since it is when "pondering her own mystery that the Church encounters the mystery of Israel." From the Christian side, the problem of Jewish-Christian relations is seen as an identity problem as much as an ecumenical one. "The very return of Christians to the sources and origins of their faith, grafted on to the earlier covenant, helps the search for unity in Christ, the cornerstone."

Where *Nostra Aetate* decries anti-Semitism, the 1975 *Guidelines* "condemns, as opposed to the very spirit of Christianity, all forms of anti-Semitism and discrimination." Where the council makes no direct reference to the Jewish-Christian joint witness to the world, the 1975 document speaks of a "Jewish and Christian tradition founded on the word of God . . . working willingly together, seeking social justice and peace on every level." Where the council presents the church as the new people of God, the *Guidelines* avoids supressionist implications and states instead: "The Old Testament and the Jewish tradition founded on it must not be set against the New Testament in such a way that the former seems to consititute a religion of only justice, fear and legalism with no appeal to the love of God and neighbor" (Deuteronomy 6:5; Leviticus 19:18).

On the promise/fulfillment theme, with which *Nostra Aetate* does not deal at all, the Vatican *Guidelines* introduce a distinction between fulfillment of the promises with the first coming of Christ and "their perfect fulfillment in his glorious return at the end of time." In preaching and in education, the Vatican *Guidelines* mandate overriding preoccupation to provide adequate background for scriptural readings "which Christians, if not well informed, might misunderstand because of prejudice," and specifies the Gospel of John and the treatment of the Pharisees as particularly important. It further emphasizes:

> Information concerning these questions is important at all levels of Christian instruction and education. Among sources of information, special attention should be paid to the following: catechisms and religious textbooks, history books, the mass media (press, radio, cinema, television).

Notes on Preaching and Catechesis, 1985

Beginning with a quotation from Pope John Paul II several years earlier, the 1985 *Notes on the Correct Way to Present the Jews and Judaism in Preaching and Catechesis in the Roman Catholic Church* asserts: "We should aim, in this field, that Catholic teaching at its different levels, in catechesis to children and young people, presents Jews and Judaism, not only in an honest and objective manner, free from prejudices and without any offenses, but also with full awareness of the heritage common" to Jews and Christians.

The *Notes* stress the "urgency and importance of precise, objective and rigorously accurate teaching on Judaism." They reaffirm the condemnation of anti-Semitism and warn that it can reappear at any time under any guise. The permanence of Israel as a historic fact is recognized in the context of God's design. Furthermore, "because of the unique relations that exist between Christanity and Judaism—linked together at the very level of their identity (John Paul II, 1982)—relations founded on the design of the God of the Covenant, the Jews and Judaism should not occupy an occasional or marginal place in catechesis: their presence there is essential and should be organically integrated."

Commenting on some issues in the Christian Scriptures the 1985 document recognizes that "references hostile or less than favorable to the Jews have their historic context in conflicts between the nascent church and the Jewish community. Certain controversies reflect Christian-Jewish relations long after the time of Jesus" (#21a). Jesus, in the Christian Scriptures, "extolled respect for the law" and "invited obedience to it" (#13). He shared "with the majority of Palestinian Jews of that time some pharisaic doctrines: the resurrection of the body; forms of piety, like alms-giving, prayer, fasting (cf. Matthew 6:1-18) and the liturgical practice of addressing God as Father; the priority of the commandment to love God and our neighbor" (cf. Mark 12:28-34).

According to the 1985 *Notes*, Christian teaching about Jews and Judaism needs to balance several pairs of ideas "which express the relation between the two economies of the Old and New Testament: promise and fulfillment, continuity and newness, singularity and universality, uniqueness and exemplary nature" (#5). The preacher, theologian and catechist need, therefore, to show that "promise and fulfillment throw light on each other; newness lies in the metamorphosis of what was there before; the singularity of the people of the Old Testament is not exclusive and is open, in the divine vision, to a universal extension; the uniqueness of the Jewish people is meant to have the force of an example" (*ibid.*).

The expression "Old Testament" appears throughout the 1985 *Notes* because "it is tradition (cf. already 2 Corinthians 3:14) but also because 'Old' does not mean 'out of date' or 'outworn' but emphasizes the *permanent* value of the Old Testament as a source of Christian Revelation" *(Dei Verbum,* 3; *Notes,* Footnote 1).

Following *Nostra Aetate* and the 1975 *Guidelines,* the 1985 *Notes* declare that the crucifixion of Jesus "cannot be blamed on all Jews then living without distinction nor upon the Jews of today . . . Christ freely underwent his passion and death because of the sins of all men." But they add that we Christians are even more responsible than "those few Jews" because we sin knowingly (#22).

Whereas *Nostra Aetate* and the 1975 *Guidelines* made no reference to the State of Israel, the 1985 *Notes* speak of a "religious attachment" between the Jewish people and the Land of Israel which "finds its roots in the biblical tradition" and which is an essential quality of Jewish covenant "fidelity to the one God" (#25). "The existence of the State of Israel" is affirmed by the 1985 *Notes* on the basis of "the common principles of international law" *(ibid.).* This affirmation warns agains "a perspective which is in itself religious" and therefore disqualifies a kind of biblical fundamentalist reading of contemporary political events in the Middle East.

Whereas *Nostra Aetate* and the 1975 *Guidelines* made no explicit acknowledgment of the validity of the ongoing Jewish witness after Christ, the 1985 *Notes* describe a continuing history of Israel after 70 CE, as "a numerous Diaspora which allowed her to carry to the whole world a witness—often heroic—of its fidelity to the one God" (#25). The very permanence of Israel is to be interpreted as part of God's design:

> The permanence of Israel (while so many ancient peoples have disappeared without trace) is a historic fact and a sign to be interpreted within God's design. We must in any case rid ourselves of the traditional idea of people *punished,* perserved as a *living argument* for Christian apologetic. It remains the chosen people.

Pope John Paul II

Both in response to the emerging tradition which began with *Nostra Aetate* and as a stimulus for further development of the tradition, Pope John Paul II has made some statements over the past several years that add to the discussion. Two of them follow.

On 17 November 1980, speaking to a Jewish community in Mainz, Germany, he described three necessary dimensions of the dialogue between Christians and Jews:

> The first dimension of this dialogue between the People of God of the Old Covenant, never revoked by God (cf. Romans 11:29), and that of the New Covenant, is at the same time a dialogue within our church, that is to say, between the first and the second part of her Bible.
>
> Second, it is important here that Christians—to continue the post-conciliar directives—should aim at understanding better the fundamental elements of the religious tradition of Judaism, and learn what fundamental lines are essential for the religious reality lived by the Jews, according to their own understanding.
>
> Third, Jews and Christians, as children of Abraham, are called to be a blessing for the world (cf. Genesis 12:2ff.) by committing themselves together for peace and justice among all men and peoples.
>
> (*L'Osservatore Romano*, 9 December 1980)

An allocution delivered by Pope John Paul on 6 March 1982 to delegates of episcopal conferences and other experts concerning the Catholic church's relations with Judaism is quoted freely in the 1985 *Notes.* One of the more frequently cited statements is:

> I myself have had occasion to say more than once: Our two communities are linked at the very level of their identities.

The pope makes the same point further on in a slightly expanded way when he says,

> Christians are on the right path, that of justice and brotherhood, when they seek, with respect and perseverance, to gather with their Semitic brethren around the common heritage which is a treasure to us all.

In another allocution in 1986, he expressed twice, first in Rome, then in Venezuela, his desire to confirm with utmost conviction that the teaching of the church proclaimed during the Second Vatican Council in the declaration *Nostra Aetate* remains always for us, for the Catholic church, a teaching which must be followed—a teaching which it is necessary to accept not merely as something fitting, but much more as an expression of the faith, an inspiration of the Holy Spirit, as a word of the divine wisdom (*SIDIC* VIII:3, 1975, p. 36).

Finally, Pope John Paul II told Australia's Jewish leaders on 26 November 1986 in Sydney, that the attitude of Catholics toward the Jewish religion "should be one of the greatest respect." "Catholics should have not only respect for Jewish people but also great fraternal love, for it is the teaching of both the Hebrew and the Christian Scriptures that the Jews are beloved of God, who has called them with an irrevocable calling."

He said "No valid theological justification could ever be found for acts of discrimination or persecution against Jews. In fact, such acts must be held to be sinful." He stressed that while religious differences between Jews and Catholics exist, cooperation is possible "in many worthy enterprises such as biblical studies and numerous works of justice and charity." Such cooperation "can bring us ever closer together in friendship and trust," he added.

Statements of popes, councils and commissions help to call attention and point direction, but the trench work remains at the local level. What happens—or doesn't happen—in parish liturgies, classrooms and catechetical discussions determines how the tradition ultimately unfolds.

Selected Bibliography

Cohn, Emil Bernhard. *This Immortal People: A Short History of the Jewish People.* Revised and expanded by Hayim Perelmuter. New York: Paulist Press, 1985.

Corner, Helga, ed. *Stepping Stones to Further Jewish-Christian Relations: An Unabridged Collection of Christian Documents.* New York: Paulist Press, 1977.

_____ ed. *More Stepping Stones to Jewish-Christian Relations: An Unabridged Collection of Christian Documents, 1975-1983.* New York: Paulist Press, 1985.

_____ and Klenicki, Leon, editors. *Issues in the Jewish-Christian Dialogue: Jewish Perspectives on Covenant, Mission and Witness.* New York: Paulist Press, 1979.

Face to Face: An Interreligious Bulletin. Published by the Anti-Defamation League of B'nai B'rith, 823 United Nations Plaza, New York NY 10017.

Fisher, Eugene. *Faith Without Prejudice.* New York: Paulist Press, 1977.

_____ "The Jewish People in Christian Preaching: A Catholic Perspective." In *The Jewish People in Christian Preaching,* edited by Darrell J. Fasching, 37-60. New York: Edwin Mellen Press, 1984.

Flannery, Austin, editor. *Vatican Council II: The Conciliar and Post Conciliar Documents.* Northport, New York: Costello Publishing Company, 1975.

Flannery, Edward H. *The Anguish of the Jews: Twenty-Three Centuries of Antisemitism.* Revised Edition. New York: Paulist Press, 1985.

Klenicki, Leon, and Huck, Gabe, editors. *Spirituality and Prayer: Jewish and Christian Understandings.* New York: Paulist Press, 1983.

Klenicki, Leon, and Wigoder, Geoffrey, editors. *A Dictionary of the Jewish Christian Dialogue.* New York: Paulist Press, 1984.

Mejia, Jorge. "Catholic Spirituality and the Challenge of Secularism." *Face to Face: An Interreligious Bulletin* 12 (Fall 1985): 25-30.

Neusner, Jacob. *A Life of Yohanan Ben Zakkai, Ca 1-80 CE.* Leiden: Brill, 1970.

_____ *First Century Judaism in Crisis.* New York: Abingdon, 1975.

_____ *The Pharisees: Rabbinic Perspectives.* New York: Ktav, 1985.

Pawlikowski, John T. *Catechetics and Prejudice: How Catholic Teaching Materials View Jews, Protestants and Racial Minorities.* New York: Paulist Press, 1973.

_____ *What Are They Saying about Christian-Jewish Relations?* New York: Paulist Press, 1980.

_____ *Christ in the Light of the Jewish-Christian Dialogue.* New York: Paulist Press, 1982.

Perrin, Norman. *Rediscovering the Teaching of Jesus.* New York: Harper & Row, 1967.

Schweitzer, Albert. *The Quest of the Historical Jesus.* New York: Macmillan, 1964.

Sloyan, Gerard. *Is Christ the End of the Law?* Philadelphia: Westminster Press, 1978.

Stendahl, Krister. *Paul Among Jews and Gentiles.* Philadelphia: Fortress Press, 1977.

_____ "The Jewish People in Christian Preaching: A Protestant Perspective." In *The Jewish People in Christian Preaching,* edited by Darrell J. Fasching, 61-76. New York: Edwin Mellen Press, 1984.

Sandmel, Samuel. *Anti-Semitism in the New Testament.* Philadelphia: Fortress Press, 1978.

_____ "Jews, Christians and the Future: What May We Hope For?" In *The Jewish People in Christian Preaching,* edited by Darrell J. Fasching, 89-104. New York: Edwin Mellen Press, 1984.

The SIDIC Review (organ of the *Service International de Documentation Judéo-Chrétienne,* Rome) is available quarterly from Dr. Eugene Fisher, Secretariat for Catholic-Jewish Relations, 1312 Massachusetts Avenue N.W., Washington DC 20005.

Thoma, Clemens. *A Christian Theology of Judaism.* New York: Paulist Press, 1980.

Werner, Eric. *The Sacred Bridge: The Interdependence of Liturgy and Music in Synagogue and Church during the First Millennium.* 2 vols. New York: Ktav, 1956, 1984.

All official Catholic documents cited in this book are available from:

The Secretariat for Catholic-Jewish Relations
National Conference of Catholic Bishops
1312 Massachusetts Avenue, N.W.
Washington DC 20005-4105